D. *Patrick Zimmerman*
Richard A. Epstein
Martin Leichtman
Maria Luisa Leichtman
Editors

D0145495

Psychotherapy in Group Care: Making Life Good Enough

Psychotherapy in Group Care: Making Life Good Enough
has been co-published simultaneously as *Residential
Treatment for Children & Youth*, Volume 20, Number 4 2003.

Pre-publication
REVIEWS,
COMMENTARIES,
EVALUATIONS . . .

"GROUNDBREAKING AND UNIQUE. . . . Provides a brilliant review of past techniques of milieu therapy and psychotherapy in residential treatment, then introduces the reader to recent developments in theory and practice based on interpersonal theory. This book is A NECESSITY FOR ALL PRACTITIONERS of residential therapy and will be an eye-opener to anyone interested in the progress and problems of psychotherapy with severely disturbed youth."

Scott Dowling, PhD
Training and Supervision Analyst
Cleveland Psychoanalytic Center
Consultant
Bellefaire Residential Treatment Center

Psychotherapy in Group Care: Making Life Good Enough

Psychotherapy in Group Care: Making Life Good Enough has been co-published simultaneously as *Residential Treatment for Children & Youth*, Volume 20, Number 4 2003.

The *Residential Treatment for Children & Youth* Monographic "Separates"

Below is a list of " separates," which in serials librarianship means a special issue simultaneously published as a special journal issue or double-issue *and* as a "separate" hardbound monograph. (This is a format which we also call a "DocuSerial.")

"Separates" are published because specialized libraries or professionals may wish to purchase a specific thematic issue by itself in a format which can be separately cataloged and shelved, as opposed to purchasing the journal on an on-going basis. Faculty members may also more easily consider a "separate" for classroom adoption.

"Separates" are carefully classified separately with the major book jobbers so that the journal tie-in can be noted on new book order slips to avoid duplicate purchasing.

You may wish to visit Haworth's website at . . .

http://www.HaworthPress.com

. . . to search our online catalog for complete tables of contents of these separates and related publications.

You may also call 1-800-HAWORTH (outside US/Canada: 607-722-5857), or Fax 1-800-895-0582 (outside US/Canada: 607-771-0012), or e-mail at:

docdelivery@haworthpress.com

Psychotherapy in Group Care: Making Life Good Enough, edited by D. Patrick Zimmerman, PsyD, Richard A. Epstein, MA, Martin Leichtman, PhD, and Maria Luisa Leichtman, PhD (Vol. 20, No. 4, 2003). *"Groundbreaking and unique. . . . Provides a brilliant review of past techniques in milieu therapy and psychotherapy in residential treatment, then introduces the reader to recent developments in theory and practice based on interpersonal theory. This book is a necessity for all practitioners of residential therapy and will be an eye-opener to anyone interested in the progress and problems of psychotherapy with severely disturbed youth." (Scott Dowling, PhD, Training & Supervision Analyst, Cleveland Psychoanalytic Center; Consultant, Bellefaire Residential Treatment Center)*

On Transitions from Group Care: Homeward Bound, edited by Richard A. Epstein, Jr., MA, and D. Patrick Zimmerman, PsyD (Vol. 20, No. 2, 2002). *Examines ways to help prepare young people for a successful transition from group care to community living.*

Innovative Mental Health Interventions for Children: Programs That Work, edited by Steven I. Pfeiffer, PhD, and Linda A. Reddy, PhD (Vol. 18, No. 3, 2001). *"An extremely valuable resource for psychologists and other mental health professionals. Clear and concise . . . strong emphasis on validation. I would recommend this book to anyone wishing to expand his/her role in treating children or anyone who now treats those with typical childhood problems but would like to do better." (David L. Wodrich, PhD, ABPP, Department of Psychology, Phoenix Children's Hospital; Clinical Associate Professor of Pediatrics, The University of Arizona Health Sciences Center)*

The Forsaken Child: Essays on Group Care and Individual Therapy, by D. Patrick Zimmerman, PsyD (Vol. 18, No. 2, 2000). *"A must read for anyone concerned about the quality of care of disturbed children and youth. Zimmerman is truly the 'great chronicler' and the 'keeper of the flame' of quality group care." (Robert B. Bloom, PhD, Executive Director, Jewish Children's Bureau, Chicago, Illinois)*

Family-Centered Services in Residential Treatment: New Approaches for Group Care, edited by John Y. Powell, PhD (Vol. 17, No. 3, 2000). *Offers suggestions and methods for incorporating parents and youths into successful treatment programs in temporary and long-term settings. This essential guide will help psychologists, therapists, and social workers unite theory and practice to create a family-oriented environment for troubled clients and provide effective services. Containing case studies, personal discoveries, and insights about the potentials and limitations of residential care, this reliable resource will help you develop improved services for youths with the help of their families using reevaluated techniques to meet individual needs.*

The New Board: Changing Issues, Roles and Relationships, edited by Nadia Ehrlich Finkelstein, MS, ACSW, and Raymond Schimmer, MAT (Vol. 16, No. 4, 1999). *This innovative book offers very specific, real life examples and informed recommendations for board management of non-profit residential service agencies and explains why and how to consider redesigning your board* *form and practice. You will explore variations of board structures, managed care pressure, increased complexity of service, reduced board member availability, and relevant theoretical discussions complete with pertinent reports on the practice of boards in the nonprofit residential service field.*

Outcome Assessment in Residential Treatment, edited by Steven I. Pfeiffer, PhD (Vol. 13, No. 4, 1996). *"Presents a logical and systematic response, based on research, to the detractors of residential treatment centers." (Canada's Children [Child Welfare League of Canada])*

Residential Education as an Option for At-Risk Youth, edited by Jerome Beker, EdD, and Douglas Magnuson, MA (Vol. 13, No. 3, 1996). *"As a remarkable leap forward, as an approach to child welfare, it is required reading for professionals–from child care workers to administrators and planners–or for anyone in search of hope for children trapped in the bitter problems of a blighted and disordered existence. . . . It is instructive, practical, and humanistic." (Howard Goldstein, DSW, Professor Emeritus, Case Western Reserve University; Author,* The Home on Gorham Street)

When Love Is Not Enough: The Management of Covert Dynamics in Organizations that Treat Children and Adolescents, edited by Donna Piazza, PhD (Vol. 13, No. 1, 1996). *"Addresses the difficult question of 'unconscious dynamics' within institutions which care for children and adolescents. The subject matter makes for fascinating reading, and anyone who has had experience of residential institutions for disturbed children will find themselves nodding in agreement throughout the book." (Emotional and Behavioural Difficulties)*

Applied Research in Residential Treatment, edited by Gordon Northrup, MD (Vol. 12, No. 1, 1995). *"The authors suggest appropriate topics for research projects, give practical suggestions on design, and provide example research reports." (Reference & Research Book News)*

Managing the Residential Treatment Center in Troubled Times, edited by Gordon Northrup, MD (Vol. 11, No. 4, 1994). *"A challenging manual for a challenging decade. . . . Takes the eminently sensible position that our failures are as worthy of analysis as our successes. This approach is both sobering and instructive." (Nancy Woodruff Ment, MSW, BCD, Associate Executive Director, Julia Dyckman Andrus Memorial, Yonkers, New York)*

The Management of Sexuality in Residential Treatment, edited by Gordon Northrup, MD (Vol. 11, No. 2, 1994). *"Must reading for residential treatment center administrators and all treatment personnel." (Irving N. Berlin, MD, Emeritus Professor, School of Medicine, University of New Mexico; Clinical Director, Child & Adolescent Services, Charter Hospital of Albuquerque; and Medical Director, Namaste Residential Treatment Center)*

Sexual Abuse and Residential Treatment, edited by Wander de C. Braga, MD, and Raymond Schimmer (Vol. 11, No. 1, 1994). *"Ideas are presented for assisting victims in dealing with past abuse and protecting them from future abuse in the facility." (Coalition Commentary [Illinois Coalition Against Sexual Assault])*

Milieu Therapy: Significant Issues and Innovative Applications, edited by Jerome M. Goldsmith, EdD, and Jacquelyn Sanders, PhD (Vol. 10, No. 3, 1993). *This tribute to Bruno Bettelheim illuminates continuing efforts to further understand the caring process and its impact upon healing and repair measures for disturbed children in residential care.*

Severely Disturbed Youngsters and the Parental Alliance, edited by Jacquelyn Sanders, PhD, and Barry L. Childress, MD (Vol. 9, No. 4, 1992). *"Establishes the importance of a therapeutic alliance with the parents of severely disturbed young people to improve the success of counseling." (Public Welfare)*

Crisis Intervention in Residential Treatment: The Clinical Innovations of Fritz Redl, edited by William C. Morse, PhD (Vol. 8, No. 4, 1991). *"Valuable in helping us set directions for continuing Redl's courageous trail-blazing work." (Reading [A Journal of Reviews and Commentary in Mental Health])*

Adolescent Suicide: Recognition, Treatment and Prevention, edited by Barry Garfinkel, MD, and Gordon Northrup, MD (Vol. 7, No. 1, 1990). *"Distills highly relevant information about the identification and treatment of suicidal adolescents into a pithy volume which will be highly accessible by all mental health professionals." (Norman E. Alessi, MD, Director, Child Diagnostic and Research Unit, The University of Michigan Medical Center)*

Psychoanalytic Approaches to the Very Troubled Child: Therapeutic Practice Innovations in Residential and Educational Settings, edited by Jacquelyn Sanders, PhD, and Barry M. Childress, MD (Vol. 6, No. 4, 1989). *"I find myself wanting to re-read the book–which I recommend for every professional library shelf, especially for directors of programs dealing with the management of residentially located disturbed youth." (Journal of American Association of Psychiatric Administrators)*

Psychotherapy in Group Care: Making Life Good Enough

D. Patrick Zimmerman, PsyD
Richard A. Epstein, MA
Martin Leichtman, PhD
Maria Luisa Leichtman, PhD
Editors

Psychotherapy in Group Care: Making Life Good Enough has been co-published simultaneously as *Residential Treatment for Children & Youth*, Volume 20, Number 4 2003.

The Haworth Press, Inc.
New York • London • Oxford

Psychotherapy in Group Care: Making Life Good Enough has been co-published simultaneously as *Residential Treatment for Children & Youth*™, Volume 20, Number 4 2003.

Cover design by Brooke R. Stiles

Library of Congress Cataloging-in-Publication Data

Psychotherapy in group care : making life good enough / D. Patrick Zimmerman . . . [et al.].
    p. cm.
    Includes bibliographical references and index.
    ISBN 0-7890-2222-2 (hard cover : alk. paper) – ISBN 0-7890-2223-0 (soft cover : alk. paper)
    1. Adolescent psychotherapy–Residential treatment. 2. Child psychotherapy–Residential treatment. I. Zimmerman, D. Patrick, Psy.D.
RJ504.5.P79 2003
616.89'14'0835–dc21   2003010629

Indexing, Abstracting & Website/Internet Coverage

This section provides you with a list of major indexing & abstracting services. That is to say, each service began covering this periodical during the year noted in the right column. Most Websites which are listed below have indicated that they will either post, disseminate, compile, archive, cite or alert their own Website users with research-based content from this work. (This list is as current as the copyright date of this publication.)

Abstracting, Website/Indexing Coverage . . . . Year When Coverage Began

- *Applied Social Sciences Index & Abstracts (ASSIA) (Online: ASSI via Data-Star) (CDRom: ASSIA Plus)*
  <www.csa.com> 1993

- *Cambridge Scientific Abstracts <www.csa.com>* 1982

- *Child Development Abstracts & Bibliography (in print and online)*
  <www.ukans.edu> 1982

- *CNPIEC Reference Guide: Chinese National Directory of Foreign Periodicals* 1995

- *Criminal Justice Abstracts* 1982

- *Educational Research Abstracts (ERA) (online database)*
  <www.tandf.co.uk/era> 2001

- *Environmental Sciences and Pollution Management (Cambridge Scientific Abstracts Internet Database Service) <www.csa.com>* . . . . . *

- *e-psyche, LLC <www.e-psyche.net>* 2001

- *Exceptional Child Education Resources (ECER) (CD/ROM from SilverPlatter and hard copy)* 1982

- *Family & Society Studies Worldwide*
  <www.nisc.com> 1996

- *IBZ International Bibliography of Periodical Literature*
  <www.saur.de> 1996

(continued)

* **Exact start date to come.**

Special Bibliographic Notes related to special journal issues (separates) and indexing/abstracting:

- indexing/abstracting services in this list will also cover material in any "separate" that is co-published simultaneously with Haworth's special thematic journal issue or DocuSerial. Indexing/abstracting usually covers material at the article/chapter level.
- monographic co-editions are intended for either non-subscribers or libraries which intend to purchase a second copy for their circulating collections.
- monographic co-editions are reported to all jobbers/wholesalers/approval plans. The source journal is listed as the "series" to assist the prevention of duplicate purchasing in the same manner utilized for books-in-series.
- to facilitate user/access services all indexing/abstracting services are encouraged to utilize the co-indexing entry note indicated at the bottom of the first page of each article/chapter/contribution.
- this is intended to assist a library user of any reference tool (whether print, electronic, online, or CD-ROM) to locate the monographic version if the library has purchased this version but not a subscription to the source journal.
- individual articles/chapters in any Haworth publication are also available through the Haworth Document Delivery Service (HDDS).

Psychotherapy in Group Care: Making Life Good Enough

CONTENTS

ABOUT THE EDITORS

D. Patrick Zimmerman, PsyD, is Assistant Director of The Sonia Shankman Orthogenic School. He is also Lecturer in the Department of Psychiatry and a member of the Committee on Human Development at The University of Chicago. He is the author of *The Forsaken Child* (Haworth) and a co-editor of the journal *Residential Treatment for Children & Youth* (Haworth).

Richard A. Epstein, MA, is Program Manager at The Sonia Shankman Orthogenic School and Lecturer at The Graham School of Continuing Education at The University of Chicago. He is managing Editor of *Residential Treatment for Children & Youth* (Haworth).

Martin Leichtman, PhD, and **Maria Luisa Leichtman, PhD,** are former Directors of Residential Treatment at The Menninger Clinic in Topeka, Kansas.

Foreword:
Psychotherapy and the Milieu:
Issues Posed for Confidentiality
and for the Therapist's Participation
in the Therapeutic Environment

The practice of psychotherapy emerged out of the medical model in both the United States and Europe over the last years of the nineteenth century. This medical model, described in some detail in Sigmund Freud's accounts of his earliest work with hysterical patents, and later expanded in his discussions of the technique of psychotherapy, assumed both confidentiality within the physician-patient relationship, and also therapeutic neutrality in the sense that the therapist did not have any decision making role in the patient's life. It was presumed that it would be difficult for a patient to talk freely about troubling issues if there was the possibility that the patient's communications would cause some reprisal in the real world outside the consulting room. More recently, even where traditions of psychotherapeutic education and practice have moved away from psychoanalysis, the confidential nature and neutrality of the patient-therapist relationship is presumed, and student therapists are counseled to avoid any discussion of their work with their clients outside of the consultation room. Some supervisors even insist that their students not use the patient's real name in order to protect the client's confidentiality.

While there can be little ethical problem regarding the confidential nature of the therapist-patient relationship (with the exception of those instances where the client's conversations indicate plans for harm to another or where there is a court order to provide a report on treatment), issues of confidentiality have al-

[Haworth co-indexing entry note]: "Foreword: Psychotherapy and the Milieu: Issues Posed for Confidentiality and for the Therapist's Participation in the Therapeutic Environment." Cohler, Bertram J. Co-published simultaneously in *Residential Treatment for Children & Youth* (The Haworth Press, Inc.) Vol. 20, No. 4, 2003, pp. xix-xxv; and: *Psychotherapy in Group Care: Making Life Good Enough* (ed: D. Patrick Zimmerman et al.) The Haworth Press, Inc., 2003, pp. xiii-xix. Single or multiple copies of this article are available for a fee from The Haworth Document Delivery Service [1-800-HAWORTH, 9:00 a.m. - 5:00 p.m. (EST). E-mail address: docdelivery@haworthpress.com].

xiii

ways been more complex when working with children. Freud himself confronted this problem with his adolescent patient Dora and her complex family situation. As Anna Freud began to develop her father's psychoanalytic model in clinical psychoanalytic work with children and adolescents, new issues of confidentiality in the treatment situation were posed.

While her chief rival, Melanie Klein (1961), maintained the standard psychoanalytic model of confidentiality in the psychoanalysis of children which was carried out in the same manner as with adults, Anna Freud (1935, 1946) believed that the child's life at school and at home made it difficult to accept this traditional psychoanalytic model. She viewed child analysis as a psycho-educational effort since children continued to live at home under the influence of their family. From the outset she recognized the importance of maintaining regular contact with parents in order both to gain additional information about the reality of her child patients' living situation and provide practical advice to parents which might foster the child's development. For example, in her analysis of one pre-adolescent boy whose parents had been divorced and who had taken up with other lovers in the flamboyant Vienna of the inter-war period (Heller, 1990), Miss Freud cautioned Peter's parents not to bring their lovers home and to recognize the impact of the parent's own lascivious activities on Peter's struggle with his own early adolescent sexuality. Her colleague August Aichhorn (1935) followed this perspective in his psychoanalytic school for so-called delinquent children in Vienna.

More recent discussions within child psychoanalysis recognize the problem regarding confidentiality when therapist and child together must deal with the reality of the child's life within the family, in school, and in the community. In the first place, many child analysts recognize that it is important to have contact with parents in order to maintain their continued support of the treatment process. In the second place, particularly when working with more troubled young people, the therapist may be called upon by the school for advice and may be asked to participate in conferences regarding the child's problems at school and at home. Most of us who work with children talk with our child patients in advance of meetings with parents or at school. We focus on the child's feelings regarding these extra-analytic contacts and while making every effort to be helpful in consultations, we avoid discussing details of the clinical material and what the child has said in sessions. Further, we report back to the child what has taken place at these meetings in order that the child will be kept informed regarding issues which are of some concern to the child, the family, and the community alike.

These problems of confidentiality and therapeutic neutrality become particularly complex when working with troubled children, adolescents, and adults in inpatient settings. Most psychodynamically oriented inpatient facilities endorse the ideology of the "therapist-administrator split" (Greenblatt, Levinson, and Williams, 1957). From this perspective, while the therapist may attend ward rounds it is understood that the therapist will not be asked to reveal details of sessions with patients or to be involved in making "real life" decisions regarding the patient's welfare in order to facilitate the patient's ease in coming to understand and resolve personal issues posed by such decisions. The therapist-administrator split means that the therapist refrains from decisions regarding the patient's life and avoids the role of messenger carrying patient requests to staff or family. The therapist is available to the patient to deal with the patient's responses to real life issues, without compromising the patient's confidentiality or autonomy. When the patient complains about decisions affecting the patient's life in the hospital or community, the therapist is able to listen and help the patient deal with these issues without having become a participant in these decisions.

At the Sonia Shankman Orthogenic School at the University of Chicago, all of these issues regarding the place of individual sessions have remained problematic. From the outset, Bettelheim (1950, 1955, 1960) maintained that symptoms were a response to a world felt by the child as overwhelming. What the School offered was a milieu in which the child was able to feel an enhanced sense of control over his or her life within a simplified environment. In contrast to the usual psychiatric hospital in which there were many staff playing different roles in the child's life, the number of different staff the child would have to deal with was much reduced. Fostering an "oak" rather than a "line" organization (Henry, 1957a, 1957b), in which there were only four kinds of staff in the child's life (the principal, teachers, counselors, and housekeeping staff), opportunities for playing one adult off against another were limited. The child was more likely to give up symptoms where the world was simplified rather than overwhelming. This treatment philosophy also meant that the child seldom encountered strangers, such as visitors, unless these visitors were announced by Bettelheim well in advance and the reason for this visit was explained to the children.

As D. Patrick Zimmerman has noted in this volume, when Bettelheim first became principal in 1945, a number of the children who had been in analysis prior to coming to the School continued their near-daily sessions, accompanied on the train downtown to these sessions by one of the two counselors responsible for a dormitory group of six to eight children. However, by 1951 he had decided that this arrangement added yet another role in the child's life and, while maintaining the therapist-administrator split, also permitted the child to keep the most painful and important issues outside of his or her experiences at the School. As a consequence, Bettelheim decided to replace these sessions outside the School with sessions at the School.

Again, consistent with his treatment philosophy, in order to maintain the child's sense of a manageable environment, children began seeing their counselors in twice or thrice weekly sessions. Counselors were generally advanced doctoral students at the University of Chicago or mental health professionals who elected to work at the School in order to learn Bettelheim's distinctive psychoanalytic treatment philosophy. These counselors were generally supervised by Bettelheim or one of two social workers who had graduated from the Child Care Program at Chicago's Institute for Psychoanalysis. However, since some children found it particularly difficult to talk with their counselors about their difficulties, a number of children were assigned to one of the two social workers for treatment.

From the outset, there was lack of clarity regarding the purpose of these sessions. Bettelheim himself never wrote or spoke about his understanding of the purpose of these sessions. Presumably, sessions took a form similar to life-space interviews in the milieu (Redl and Wineman, 1951, 1952) in which troubling issues could be dealt with between a staff member and a child soon after the confrontation had taken place. However, sessions were also presumed to foster personality reconstruction as Bettelheim (1950, 1955) had portrayed this process. While this arrangement did further reduce the number of adults with whom the child was involved, it posed serious problems regarding both confidentiality and therapeutic neutrality. Counselor-therapists were frequently called upon at staff meetings to make decisions about issues in the child's life, such as the therapeutic justification for a home visit based both on information obtained in individual sessions and also life in the dormitory and classroom. From the child's perspective, it was difficult to come to session and talk about painful issues raised with another child or a counselor in the milieu when the therapist was both that child's counselor and necessarily involved in the child's daily life, and perhaps also seeing other children in treatment from that same dormitory. Issues raised in sessions frequently found their way into dormitory conversations, just as conflicts between the young person and the counselor in the dormitory found their way into the therapeutic situation.

Counselor-therapists were often in the position of having to see a child in a session in the aftermath of some situation in the dormitory where that counselor and therapist had been involved with the child in a disciplinary issue such as the child's failure to get to breakfast on time, or a quarrel between the child and another children in the dormitory or classroom. The counselor-therapist then had to deal with his or her own feelings about these situations. More than countertransference was involved. Confrontations in the milieu often led to harsh words on the part of both children and their counselors. The children referred to the Orthogenic School had most often failed out of all conventional treatment modalities. Often externalizing their psychological distress, they posed continuing clinical management problems in the dormitory. Acutely sensitive to the feelings of their counselors and teachers, these troubled young people continually confronted staff with issues personally painful for a staff member working with these children. Indeed, many of the staff themselves elected to begin psychotherapy as a result of working with these troubled young people. Coming to session with a child following a particularly tense situation the preceding morning in the dormitory in which the counselor-therapist's competence was directly challenged, it was often difficult to listen to a child's complaints and help the child to understand his or her own role in some difficult issue within the dormitory group.

The papers in the present volume address this issue of the place of psychotherapy within the milieu and deal with the twin issues of confidentiality together with the implications for the treatment situation when the therapist is necessarily a real person with decision making authority in the child's life. These papers report on the interplay of staff work in sessions within the milieu in two well-known residential treatment programs, the Orthogenic School and the Menninger Clinic. The authors of the papers reporting on the Orthogenic School, D. Patrick Zimmerman and Richard A. Epstein, are senior staff members at the School. Responsible for admissions to the School (at the present time, psychodynamically oriented psychotherapy is carried out by several staff psychologists and advanced students in psychiatry and psychology working under supervision rather than by dormitory counselors), Zimmerman is in a somewhat less complex situation than Epstein who has administrative responsibility for some of the young people he sees in sessions. The three papers by the Leichtmans deal directly with the manner in which individual psychotherapy provided by senior therapists can be integrated within the milieu and accompanying problems regarding confidentiality. While the model for the Orthogenic School is that of a somewhat longer-term treatment program, the program at the Menninger Clinic recently has focused on shorter-term psychotherapy during a time-limited inpatient stay and primarily addresses issues of support prior to return to the community.

Following the revised model of inpatient treatment at the Menninger Clinic's children's treatment program, the therapist is a senior staff member who may have administrative as well as clinical responsibility for the children seen in treatment. The treatment model at the Orthogenic School has evolved from one in which advanced doctoral students planning on a career in psychoanalysis and education served as both counselor and therapist to a model in which there are childcare staff and a several senior mental health professionals seeing children in expressive, intensive, medium- to long-term psychotherapy. However, in each setting there are issues regarding the role of the therapist in the day-to-day life issues affecting the young person's life outside of the treatment situation. The Leichtmans note in their papers that, inevitably, practical problems regarding the confidentiality of the young person's communication in psychotherapy will enter into the situation outside the consulting room.

In one of their discussions, the Leichtmans suggest that the important issue is not the confidentiality of the patient's communications but rather maintaining an atmosphere of trust which is best achieved by talking honestly with patients about how information from sessions might be used and then letting young people decide what they will choose to reveal. At the very least, open communication fosters enhanced sense of autonomy for young people deciding what and why they reveal painful issues within the psychotherapeutic situation. Further, since therapy is necessarily time-limited in the Menninger program, therapists focus largely on "real life" problems which young people may confront as they return to the community. Confidentiality is, however, maintained within the treatment team, which also offers both the therapist and other members of the team opportunities to deal with their own feelings evoked by work with these troubled young people.

The papers included in this collection reflect the very best and most sophisticated present work on the integration of individual and milieu therapy working with children and adolescents within an inpatient setting. These papers carefully address issues regarding the place of the individual therapist within the total treatment program, problems posed as the therapist is also responsible for real life decision making among young people seen in sessions, and the meaning of confidentiality with an inpatient setting. As these papers show, there are no easy answers to these questions. Rather, staff make a number of complex compromises founded on the needs of the particular young persons with whom they are working, always recognizing the importance of the therapist's own feelings in working with these patients as a factor relevant in making such real-world decisions as placements following an inpatient stay, timing and duration of home visits, and granting particular privileges based on best current understanding of what would most facilitate therapeutic progress within the inpatient setting.

Bertram J. Cohler, PhD
The University of Chicago

REFERENCES

Aichhorn, A. (1935/1965). *Wayward youth.* New York: Viking Press.

Bettelheim, B. (1950). *Love is not enough: The treatment of emotionally disturbed children.* Glencoe, IL (New York): The Free Press/Macmillan.

Bettelheim, B. (1955). *Truants from life: The rehabilitation of emotionally disturbed children.* Glencoe, IL (New York): Free Press/Macmillan.

Bettelheim, B. (1960). *The informed heart: Autonomy in a mass age.* Glencoe, IL (New York): The Free Press/Macmillan.

Freud, A. (1935/1963). *Psychoanalysis for teachers and parents: Introductory lectures* (Trans. B. Low). Boston: Beacon Press.

Freud, A. (1946/1964). *The psychoanalytical treatment of children: Lectures and essays.* New York: Schocken Books.

Greenblatt, M., Levinson, D.J., & Williams, R.H. (Eds.) (1957). *The patient and the mental hospital: Contributions of research in the science of human behavior.* Glencoe, IL (New York): The Free Press/Macmillan.

Heller, P. (1990). *A child analysis with Anna Freud* (Revised Edition) (Trans. S. Burkhardt and M. Weigand). Madison, CT: The International Universities Press.

Henry, J. (1957a). Types of institutional structure, *Psychiatry, 20,* 47-60.

Henry, J. (1957b). The culture of interpersonal relations in a therapeutic institution for emotionally disturbed children, *American Journal of Orthopsychiatry, 27,* 725-734.

Klein, M. 1961). *Narrative of a child analysis: The conduct of the psycho-analysis of children as seen in the treatment of a ten year old boy.* New York: Basic Books.

Redl, F., & Wineman, D. (1951/1966). *Children who hate: The disorganization and breakdown of behavior controls.* New York: The Free Press/Macmillan.

Redl, F., & Wineman, D. (1952/1966). *Controls from within: Techniques for the treatment of the aggressive child.* New York: The Free Press/Macmillan.

Preface:
Child and Milieu:
Tensions Between Group
and Individual Care

In terms of addressing the tensions inherent in the early attempts to provide individual psychotherapy for young persons within a group care setting, Bruno Bettelheim was one of the pioneers who through the years grappled with the many issues involved in this effort. Regarding the child most appropriate for residential treatment at a facility such as the Orthogenic School, Bettelheim at first proposed that milieu therapy alone was the treatment of choice both for children whose ability to maintain contact with parental figures had been catastrophically destroyed, as well as for those children who apparently had not acquired the tools for establishing such a relationship in the first place (Bettelheim and Sylvester, 1949). This emphasis upon the overiding importance of the effects of the milieu in general was also emphasized somewhat later in Trieschman, Whittaker, and Brendtro's classic study, *The Other 23 Hours: Childcare Work with Emotionally Disturbed Children* (1959).

According to Bettelheim, milieu therapy was most indicated where the basic needs of the child had been so neglected that the child, in Bettelheim's view, lacked psychological integration at even the pregenital level of development (according to the then prevalent classical psychosexual and ego psychology drive-theory models of treatment). For children who had achieved a higher level of integration, presenting more neurotic disturbances, psychotherapy alone might be indicated (for example, in situations where a disturbance in the Oedipal phase occasioned a regression to earlier developmental stages as a point of fixation). In such instances, Bettelheim felt, an interpersonal relation-

[Haworth co-indexing entry note]: "Preface: Child and Milieu: Tensions Between Group and Individual Care." Zimmerman, D. Patrick. Co-published simultaneously in *Residential Treatment for Children & Youth* (The Haworth Press, Inc.) Vol. 20, No. 4, 2003, pp. xxvii-xxxiii; and: *Psychotherapy in Group Care: Making Life Good Enough* (ed: D. Patrick Zimmerman et al.) The Haworth Press, Inc., 2003, pp. xxi-xxvii. Single or multiple copies of this article are available for a fee from The Haworth Document Delivery Service [1-800-HAWORTH, 9:00 a.m. - 5:00 p.m. (EST). E-mail address: docdelivery@haworthpress.com].

xxi

ship with a psychotherapist alone could be anticipated to develop and to help in resolving the prior traumatization.

In another attempt to specify his understanding of the milieu, Bettelheim described what he understood to be the most important differences between individual psychiatric treatment and milieu care (Bettelheim, 1949). First, he pointed out that the then prevalent psychiatric techniques had been developed in treating adults, concentrating on uncovering the repressed and changing deviate personality structures. However, Bettelheim believed that for those children most in need of residential milieu treatment, emotional difficulties stemmed both from their basic inability to organize their personalities in the first place and from a near *absence* of repressive defensive mechanisms. According to Bettelheim, "the psychiatric school's therapeutic task is to bring order into chaos rather than to reorganize a deviately put together cosmos" (Bettelheim, 1949, p. 91). In other words, whereas the traditional or classical model of individual psychiatric treatment often aimed toward permitting greater instinctual gratification by lifting repression, the education of the psychiatric school was aimed more toward the socialization of wild, overpowering instinctual tendencies. Bettelheim's position regarding repression was somewhat reversed a few years later when he began writing about infantile autism, where the amelioration of the effects of massive and dysfunctional repression became one of the *aims* of his theory of treatment for the autistic child.

Second, in Bettelheim's view, the prevalent schools of psychiatry in his time regarded the transference relationship, specifically the development of the transference neurosis, and its exploration and resolution, as the major ingredient of successful individual psychodynamic treatment, presupposing the previous existence of important relationships, feelings about which could be transferred onto the therapist. He concluded that children needing milieu treatment characteristically had experienced *no* relationships that were suitable as a vehicle for transference. This led to Bettelheim's belief that residential treatment should be largely focused on the present, on the promotion of ego strengths in the context of daily living tasks. Therefore, according to Bettelheim, milieu therapy should be most attentive to experiences in the present, while individual psychotherapy was more appropriately concerned with events from the past. A "psychiatric residential school" needed to be much more concerned with helping the child order the world of the present, while psychiatric treatment was seen as more concerned with doing away with misinterpretations of past experiences. In Bettelheim's milieu setting, "instead of reliving the pathogenic past, the child is helped to live successfully in the present. Convincing demonstrations of ego strength thus take the place of speculation about the possible sources of its weaknesses" (Bettelheim, 1949, p. 93). Again, this was a hypothesis that Bettelheim later seemed to modify when he wrote more specifically about the treatment of autistic children (Bettelheim, 1967).

Bettelheim gave considerable attention to the issue of the relationship and tension between individual psychotherapy and milieu therapy in the residential setting, but his writings about this treatment issue tended to be somewhat contradictory and equivocal. This tension between individual and group care persists in the treatment setting of the Orthogenic School, an as yet unresolved polarity which may be characteristic of residential treatment centers in general. Initially, Bettelheim seemed to dismiss the usefulness of individual therapy in residential care on the basis of clinical assumptions about the kinds of problems presented by children he deemed most appropriate for residential treatment. To recapitulate, Bettelheim felt that individual psychotherapy, as he understood it, was characterized by the lifting of repressions, the development of transference in the treatment relationship, and a predominant focus upon the past. These elements of individual psychotherapy seemed to make individual treatment incompatible with milieu therapy, which aimed to strengthen ego controls over unmodulated impulses and was more attentive to life in the present.

Nevertheless, despite Bettelheim's arguments that individual psychotherapy had little to offer for children in need of residential treatment, such treatment was in fact formally provided to some children at the Orthogenic School during its early years, both within the school and by therapists outside the school. For example, one of the earliest examples of the richly detailed case studies of children at the school appears to be based upon insights derived from a boy's individual psychotherapy sessions at the school, possibly with Dr. Emmy Sylvester (Bettelheim and Sylvester, 1950). In fact, the clarity and persuasiveness of that particular study's narrative style was later to become a model for Bettelheim's later reconstructive case studies of delinquent, schizophrenic, and autistic children. In *Love Is Not Enough* (1950), his first book about the school, Bettelheim appeared to moderate his position against psychotherapy in the milieu, noting that "somewhere along the line of his rehabilitation . . . [the child] . . . must learn to form and manage more lasting, more intense and mature relations than those he can form within the group" (1950, p. 243).

The child *did* need, it turned out, the experience of a private, long-term relationship with an adult to clear away "the residues of the more distant past." However, while the "so-called individual sessions" had many things in common with child psychotherapy, Bettelheim felt that they had functions which, in his view, exceeded those usually provided by traditional forms of psychotherapy, including the provision of a private setting for the discharge of strong aggression and negativism (rather than in the group setting), to allow regressive behaviors, and to provide educative guidance for acquiring basic social interaction skills.

The individual sessions also clearly differed from classical forms of psychotherapy in other ways, including: (1) the use of staff members who had little or no formal training in the provision of psychotherapy as "individual session" persons, and (2) the very close interrelation between the individual treatment experience and the reality of group life (for example, a staff person might have served both as a child's group counselor and as the individual session person). However, by providing his model of private sessions, Bettelheim was attempting to resolve the seeming differences between individual and milieu therapy by the compromise of offering "individual sessions" which had some commonalities to individual child therapy, but which in many ways seemed to be quite different from formal individual psychotherapy.

PERSISTING DISCREPANCIES
BETWEEN INDIVIDUAL AND GROUP CARE

Despite Bettelheim's efforts to deal with this polarity of individual versus milieu therapy in the residential treatment setting, the tension between the two modes of treatment was never clearly resolved. This difficulty is revealed even today in the persistence of a number of treatment issues. At a more theoretical level, a number of factors may contribute to the tension between individual and group care in the residential setting. First, even within a cohesive psychodynamic group milieu, one might find individual therapists providing a wide range of sometimes-divergent forms of psychodynamic psychotherapy, ranging from classical drive and ego one-person psychologies to some of the more contemporary approaches. Further, especially given the time-constraints of current residential funding sources, one might speculate that more therapists today are turning to shorter-term, more reality-oriented treatment approaches, with an increase in the use of the behavioral and cognitive-behavior perspectives.

Even given the potential diversity of approaches in individual therapy, it is highly likely that the individual model of treatment is a one-person psychology model, with assumptions that are divergent from, or logically incompatible with, the intrinsically interpersonal life of the residential setting. In addition, this kind of difficulty can be further aggravated when both the individual treatment *and* the milieu setting are seen only through the lens of the one-person psychology model, in effect systematically invalidating the residents' real perceptions that their "world" in the treatment center is essentially a two-person, interpersonal experience, potentially nullifying their sense of credibility and self-worth. Again, as proposed in the previous section, promoting a two-person or even constructivist approach in the understanding of both the individual and group care experiences of the residents is essential when possible, and where this is not feasible it is crucial to strive for some integration of the one/two person dichotomies in the general treatment setting.

In settings which pose fundamental obstacles to efforts at integration of those dichotomies, Altman (1993, 1995) has extended the two-person relational model of individual therapy to a broader, hypothetical "three-person" model, where the third person in the individual treatment process represents the context of the socioeconomic status of the patient, as well as the institutional characteristics of the treatment setting. For Altman, his three-person model further enables the therapist to recognize, for example, the external setting for individual relational treatment (in his case, an inner-city public mental health clinic) as an analytic issue, rather than simply as an interference with the more traditional model of two people working in isolation from the reality of the institutional arrangements which surround them, or (in terms of the issues presented in this paper) from the impact of a milieu based upon clinical assumptions which are divergent from the two-person model of treatment.

Complicating the theoretical issues facing the provision of individual psychotherapy within group care settings (and there are surely many more) are a number of practical difficulties. For example, in addition to the fact that a wide variety of theoretical individual therapy orientations may be provided in the same residential treatment setting, direct-care workers in the milieu often lack formal training in or a personal experience with individual psychotherapy. On the one hand, this situation can subtly dispose individual therapists to feel and/or act as though they possess a higher, special, more powerful understanding of the patient or resident, a stance which can result in direct-care staff feeling as though they are viewed as naive and expected to simply passively cooperate with the authority and special "expertise" of the individual psychotherapist. On the other hand, even if an individual therapist emphasizes to direct-care staff the ongoing *uncertainty* of the individual therapy process, the direct-care staff could still react to personal feelings about their own lack of formal training or direct experience with an unrealistically "magical" view of the process of individual psychotherapy, feelings of suspicion and fear, or a sense of barely disguised mistrust. These reactions can be directed not only to the individual therapist's work, but also displaced onto the youth's own experience of his/her involvement in the individual therapy process.

Additional tension between the individual psychotherapy and the general milieu can arise from the fact that it can be extremely difficult for the individual therapist to richly convey the details of the techniques and interactional fabric of the individual therapy experience to other staff members in the group setting. This dilemma is seen not only in the ongoing daily life of the milieu, but it is also reflected in the general body of literature on residential treatment, where over the years there has been a striking paucity of published extended case material describing the *actual conduct* of individual psychotherapy with children in the residential milieu. Another obstacle to harmony between individual and milieu therapy is created by the sometimes subtle, though often overt belief that individual therapy is mostly involved with the child's inner life, while milieu therapy is more concerned with experiences with others and the external milieu environment. This is, of course, another reflection of the illusory one-person/two-person psychology dichotomy. The reality is that *each* treatment modality is involved with *both* inner and outer aspects of the child's experiences, which may serve to make a resolution of the tension between the two kinds of treatment even *more* difficult in practice.

Other practical issues which emerge as a reflection of this polarity between the individual and group or milieu treatment modalities in residential care include the issue of confidentiality and trust in the individual therapy relationship conducted within a larger group care setting committed to all-staff communication. There can also occur instances of the periodic blurring of boundaries between the seemingly more transference-driven individual treatment and the child's sometimes more reality-oriented experiences of the milieu group life. Another difficulty, again related to the seeming individual/group polarity, is the periodic emergence of discrepant treatment goals for a particular child (such as rapid behavioral change versus longer-term internal growth), which can be provoked by milieu direct-care workers' understandable wishes to see a child's disruptive behaviors in the group setting quickly diminish through individual therapy interventions. The foregoing dilemmas are, of course, only an illustrative sample of the many difficult complexities that can arise between the individual and group care treatment efforts in residential settings. The following collection of papers attempts to address many of the theoretical and practical issues described above, through a review of classical case material, presentation of contemporary psychotherapy case studies, and current discussions of the practical and theoretical aspects of providing individual psychotherapy in the residential treatment setting.

D. Patrick Zimmerman, PsyD
The Sonia Shankman Orthogenic School
at The University of Chicago

REFERENCES

Altman, N. (1993). Psychoanalysis and the urban poor. *Psychoanalytic Dialogues, 3* (1), 29-49.

Altman, N. (1995). *The Analyst in the Inner City: Race, Class, and Culture Through a Psychoanalytic Lens.* Hillsdale NJ/London: The Analytic Press.

Bettelheim, B. (1949). A psychiatric school. *Quarterly Journal of Child Behavior,* 1, 86-95.

Bettelheim, B. (1950). *Love Is Not Enough.* New York: Free Press.

Bettelheim, B. (1967). *The Empty Fortress.* New York: Free Press.

Bettelheim, B., & Sylvester, E. (1949). Milieu therapy: Indications and illustrations. *Psychoanalytic Review,* 36, 54-68.

Bettelheim, B., & Sylvester, E. (1950). Delinquency and morality. *The Psychoanalytic Study of the Child,* 5, 329-342. New York: International Universities Press.

Trieschman, A., Whittaker, J., & Brendtro, L. (1969). *The Other 23 Hours: Childcare Work with Emotionally Disturbed Children.* Chicago: Aldine Publishing Company.

Is Life Good Enough?
A Close Race to Make It Better

D. Patrick Zimmerman, PsyD

SUMMARY. This paper presents certain aspects of the analytic process that emerged in work with an adolescent boy who, for lack of better diagnostic specificity, had come to feel as though he was a psychological orphan. The relational perspective of the analytic process described in this short report included comments about the boy's incessant protest and complaints, his ongoing expressions of rage, his feelings of hope and dread in an intimate relationship, our mutual feelings of affection, and aspects of conducting analytic work within a residential therapeutic environment experienced by the boy as non-responsive to his needs. The paper described how viewing his rageful outbursts in the treatment sessions as a special protest of desperate hope, with an optimistic view of the boy's psychic future, enabled me to view the targets of his rage in part as intensified reflections of his own despairing feelings of vulnerability and helplessness. The latter included his strong conviction that he

---

The author may be written at: The Sonia Shankman Orthogenic School at The University of Chicago, 1365 East 60th Street, Chicago, IL 60637 (E-mail: pzimmerm@midway.uchicago.edu).

The author wishes to acknowledge deep gratitude to Irwin Z. Hoffman, PhD (Chicago), for his valuable discussions about and contributions to this paper.

A version of this paper has been published in *The Journal of Infant, Child and Adolescent Psychotherapy* (The Other Press, copyright 2003).

was learning disabled, feelings of being unable to experience that other people really had any genuine desire to give him anything, his relative inability to really grasp and contain the idea of psychic conflict, and little understanding that others' perspectives could be of any use for him. The presentation concluded with some brief comments about the beginning steps of progress that were made by this adolescent boy in his attempts to reach out and establish relationships with others, as painful as that might have been for him. *[Article copies available for a fee from The Haworth Document Delivery Service: 1-800-HAWORTH. E-mail address: <docdelivery@ haworthpress.com> Website: <http://www.HaworthPress.com> © 2003 by The Haworth Press, Inc. All rights reserved.]*

KEYWORDS. Relational psychoanalysis, residential treatment, group care, child development, adolescent development, paradox, metaphor, hope, interpretation

INTRODUCTION

This case report describes analytic work with an adolescent boy who, for lack of better diagnostic specificity, presented with pervasive feelings of being a psychological orphan. The brief aspects of analytic process described in this short report of work with this boy range from comments about his incessant protest and complaints, expressions of rage, feelings of hope and dread in an intimate relationship (Mitchell, 1993), mutual feelings of affection, and aspects of conducting analytic work within a residential therapeutic environment experienced by the boy as constricting and unempathic.

In particular, coming to feel like an orphan, or like a psychological orphan, may have much to do with the loss of a beloved one, feelings of being unloved, or feelings of being unworthy to be loved. At certain points of work with the boy described in this case, the issue of feelings of tender affection came briefly to the forefront, baring its heart in our work together with sometimes startling, surprising openness. While the issue of expressed caring feelings was not belabored at length in the treatment nor in the account of the case which follows in this paper, it is useful to note here the presence of this element of mutually affectionate feeling, if only to underscore its emergence as a striking contrast to the pervasive tone of anger and sadness that is contained in most of this boy's case description.

TENSIONS BETWEEN INDIVIDUAL TREATMENT
AND RESIDENTIAL CARE

The Milieu and a Three-Person Treatment Perspective

The analytic work that is reported with the boy in this case study was conducted at the Sonia Shankman Orthogenic School, a residential treatment center for children and adolescents at the University of Chicago. Given the pervasive influence of residential life upon individual therapy, it is useful to describe some of the tensions that can arise between individual treatment and the social context of group care in the residential setting. Despite the awareness that one of the contexts of our actions is always *"the context of ignorance of contexts"* (Hoffman, 1998, p. 76), Altman has proposed that there is some potential value to a shift from the contemporary two-person model of treatment to a "three person model." In his discussion, the third "person" represents the social context of the treatment, which includes "the analytic significance of the racial, cultural, and social class status of patient and analyst, as well as the institutional context of their work" (Altman, 1995, p. 56).

The influence of the milieu in residential treatment, especially a milieu experienced as potentially or actually disruptive, cannot be split off from or disowned in the work of individual treatment within a group care setting and must be viewed within the kind of third-person context described by Altman. It is probably true that Altman's conceptualization of a three-person psychology as it relates to residential treatment has been a phenomenon that analytic practitioners of differing theoretical orientations have been aware of for years. Nevertheless, the issue as raised in this paper is a matter of a degree of emphasis, and Altman's model serves to bring this issue clearly to the forefront in treatment conducted in settings such as residential treatment facilities. In addition, his formulation is more explicit about the relational implications of this three-person perspective.

Qualitatively, this involves a clear acknowledgement that the analyst is involved also and that the analyst/patient interactions are influenced by the embeddedness in the external setting. This is especially important when the patient (such as in this case report) perceives the treatment environment as negative and depriving, and an important issue for the analyst is to find a way to function as a good object within the bad environment, as well as to be thoughtful about what the children bring to treatment in their complaints about the larger treatment environment. At the same time, there is the very real possibility that the child's view of the bad environment description also serves as an illustration of the child's opinion or feeling that my being part of the environment makes *me* bad as well.

On "Splitting": Transference Distortion versus Reality

It is always the case that one should be attentive to the possibility that the patient may be resorting to defensive splitting in the residential treatment environment, an issue that has been noted by a number of writers (Borowitz, 1970; Bullard, 1990; Redl & Wineman, 1951; Rinsley, 1974, 1980). However, since the notion of "splitting" has become so commonplace in terms of describing a particular kind of behavior exhibited by some young persons in residential care, it is useful to go further than simply to name the behavior, and instead to examine it somewhat more closely. For example, one should investigate whether the term "splitting" refers to a tendency to defensively foster conflict to thwart the external representatives of the treatment process, or whether the "splitting" has an intrapsychic dynamic of a less obvious nature. On the other hand, does the use of the term "splitting" serve to lay all of the blame upon the patient, along with an assumption that the patient's view of things is simply a distortion of the real situation? In that case, what is called "splitting" may serve to avoid an acknowledgement that the patient's assessment of the treatment situation may in fact be an accurate one.

As one example of "splitting" behavior as potentially based upon a patient's *objective* perceptions, rather than simply the patient's transferential distortions, Rinsley (1980) wrote about one of his patient's "splitting" responses in the presence of an aggressive, driving, obsessional new psychiatric resident. As a reaction to her mounting terror of his driving aggressiveness, she attempted to create Rinsley as the "all good" doctor to ward off the new resident, whom she perceived to be a potentially frightening attacker. Eventual reassignment of the new resident to another ward was associated with a gradual upward trend in the patient's clinical condition.

In terms of the adolescent in this case report, many of his complaints about staff members and the milieu appeared to have some merit. In a sense, working with children and adolescents in this type of situation is like doing individual treatment with outpatients with bad homes, only now you're *both* inside the bad home. Students will often take their rage about the injuries and deprivations that they suffer and turn it against themselves, to show to everyone the damage that's being done. It's like they're saying, "No one is noticing all of the bad drivers that I see, so I'll jaywalk so that I'll get hit and badly hurt, then maybe people will notice." One key to mental health in this difficult situation is for the patient to *forego* the urge for revenge. The therapist must advocate for constructive living under bad conditions, promote the ability to find pockets of good in their daily lives, rather than sulking all of the time about what's bad. There are *always* "seams" in every bad system. What is required is to be able to "leap" out of the system and make a gesture toward someone. This requires a real sense of creativity in confronting the issue of how to get the good experience to outweigh the depriving environment, metaphorically like the plants managing to grow in the rocks of the desert. The issue is an environment that is experienced as too toxic versus a rich intrapsychic interest. All of this is even harder in the individual treatment because the patient comes to feel that the bad things are in *my* house, and it looks like I'm the parent that stands by and lets them happen.

THEORETICAL COMMENTS

Multiple Perspectives on Developmental Theory

The following discussion of the analytic treatment with a highly agitated and depressed young adolescent boy in residential care is a presentation of highly selective analytic process material. The author is aware that this material could well have been organized from various one-person psychology perspectives, such as drive, ego, self, or traditional relational theoretical positions. Over the years, each of those perspectives has proposed a range of developmental models of adolescence, including the psychosexual model (S. Freud, 1905/1962; Jones, 1922/1948), the drive/ego psychology model (A. Freud, 1958; Blos, 1962, 1979), the psychosocial model (Erikson, 1950, 1959, 1968), the self-psychology model (Wolf, 1980; Kohut, 1971, 1972, 1977), and earlier object-relations models (Jacobson, 1954, 1961, 1964; Mahler, 1952, 1971, 1972, 1975; Mahler & Furer, 1968). For others, those more interested in cognitive development, it includes an alliance with Piagetian theory (Piaget, 1975) or, more recently, the developmental acquisition of "mentalization or reflective function" (Fonagy & Target, 1998).

Elsewhere, the variety of developmental tasks and achievements associated with many of those theories have been elaborated in some detail (Zimmerman, 1990), including the reworking of oedipal issues, a second process of separation-individuation, the achievement of a sense of ego identity and capacity for intimacy, the achievement of a capacity for abstract and "formal" thought processes, the establishment of a renewed cohesive sense of self, and the renegotiations of self-object representations. More recently, distinguished from the focus upon separation-individuation, the work of Stern (1985) has emphasized a movement from an early sense of autonomy to a later capacity for interpersonal connection and mutuality, while Benjamin (1995) proposed a line of development leading to a sense of mutual "recognition," based upon the capacity to sustain an ever-present sense of *tension* between separation and interpersonal mutuality.

In my own work with children and adolescents, I have found that particular theories of motivation and development are indeed valuable in helping to identify or formulate various interactions and experiences that come to the foreground at different times in the treatment process. While theorists have differed with regard to the developmental issues or tasks that they believe are most important to be mastered, I do not feel compelled to favor a particular theory in order to benefit from the specific account of development that each theorist considers pivotal or fundamental. In this sense, I tend to agree with Hoffman's (1987) description of a position favoring a more integrative stance regarding developmental theories:

> In the course of my work I find myself drawing upon a variety of theories to help make sense of the patient's communications. In succession, or sometimes in combinations that are concurrent, I may find it helpful to think in terms of the difficulties associated with sexual differences and the Oedipal complex as described by Freud, the ramifications of envy as described by Melanie Klein, the need for acknowledgement and appreciation from others as well as the need for others who are admired as described by Kohut, the struggles over separation and individuation as described by Mahler, and so on. Although one or another of these issues may seem more prominent in the case of one patient than another, I do not find it necessary or desirable to commit myself to a formulation as to what is primary and what is secondary in any particular case or even at any particular moment with a patient. . . . The more openness there is to various theoretical perspectives and languages, the more likely it will be that what the patient and the analyst resist formulating at one moment will be put into words and articulated at a later time. (p. 211)

Relational Concepts in Adolescent Treatment

Presenting this case ultimately led to making choices between emphasizing the selection of material that illustrated particular examples of dialectical thinking and participation in the boy's treatment, and an organization that attempted to more clearly capture the anguished tone pervading the ongoing development and progress of the treatment. Given the relative paucity of extended accounts of the analytic process with adolescents in recent years, the case material presented here tends to stress the latter. Nevertheless, this stance was assumed in the hope that the reader would still be able to discern the strong interactive nature and conversational tone of this case, since the dialectical-constructivist model is implicitly embedded as a crucial aspect of the ongoing treatment experience with this boy (Ghent, 1992, 1995; Gill, 1994; Hoffman, 1994, 1998; Mitchell, 1993, 1997; Stern, 1997).

While some might voice concern that the authors cited above in support of the contemporary relational perspective proposed have worked largely with adults, it should be noted that the historical thread of this treatment approach leads back to clinicians who actually did much of their work with children, or who were deeply involved in developing theories which reflected issues related to child development (Ferenczi, 1913/1952, 1931/1955; Fairbairn, 1952; Klein, 1932, 1959; Winnicott, 1958, 1965). Further, in recent years there has been a growing recognition that for some time analytic work with young people has been moving toward a relational model of theory and practice, and that it is this very movement which addresses many of the difficulties that earlier theorists encountered in doing analytic work with children and adolescents, difficulties that seemed to call for substantial "modifications" in the treatment of young people (Altman, 1994; Frankel, 1998). Frankel (1998) has argued that the essential processes of analytic therapy are *fully* present in child therapy (and by inference adolescent therapy) and often may be seen more clearly there than in adult therapy. Among those processes, he includes the capacity for the provisional attitude of play and the renegotiations of self-other relationships.

While it is beyond the scope of this paper to elaborate fully upon the details of the theoretical perspective represented in the analytic work with this boy, it is useful to mention a few of those aspects, particularly some of those which have emerged to create a sense of deviation from the traditional treatment stance which had appeared to be technically correct as an essential part of a therapeutic effect. First, there has been the emergent tradition involving the constructive use, even expression, of countertransference (Bollas, 1987; Ehrenberg, 1992; Gill, 1982; Hoffman, 1998; Levenson, 1983; Modell, 1990; Racker, 1968; Searles, 1965; Stolorow & Atwood, 1992). Although those authors generally reflect work with adult patients, this tradition also has been represented in work with children and adolescents (Borowitz, 1970; Colm, 1966; Ekstein, Wallerstein, & Mandelbaum, 1992; Greene, 1972; Rinsley, 1980). Given the recognition of the potential for constructive use of countertransference feelings, however, this author agrees with Hoffman's position that "each instance of use or expression of countertransference [needs] to be examined individually to weigh the relative contributions of therapeutic, nontherapeutic, and antitherapeutic factors (1998, p. 195). Nevertheless, Hoffman proposes that there is quite possibly something about the deviation itself, regardless of its particular content, that has therapeutic potential, at the very least in terms of the patient having reason to feel recognized in a special, authentic way.

Second, although there is current emphasis upon the acknowledgment and constructive use of the analyst's emotional participation in the treatment process, in a certain way analytic restraint continues to be crucial for therapeutic practice. On the one hand, such discipline does provide restrictions on the extent and kind of analyst involvement, standing as the background for the spontaneous, interpersonal experiences of the treatment participants. However, to the degree that analysts allow themselves to be affected and known by their patients, the restrictions of analytic discipline are probably more qualified than they once were in the past.

Closely aligned to this issue of spontaneity versus discipline is the interplay between the stance of mutuality and the stance of asymmetry. This interplay implies an ongoing dialectic, even tension, between the patient's perception of the analyst as a person like him/herself and the patient's perception of and need for the analyst as a person with specially acquired knowledge, judgment skills, and even power. What the balance should be between asymmetry and mutuality at any particular instance, or over the longer term, is difficult to know, and the struggle to achieve this sense of balance is always attended by "a sense of struggle with uncertainty" (Hoffman, 1998, p. 204). So in addition to the fact that the analyst is always implicated in co-creating what the patient experiences in treatment, he or she must always struggle with a sense of uncertainty about whatever he or she chooses to do.

This struggle may well be what is at the very core of what it means to be a new and benevolent object for the patient, because it is a stance which is the most open to the large number of as yet unelaborated potentials within the patient and the analyst. It assumes that analytic therapists can safely presume that they do not necessarily have a special access to their own motives, nor are they always able, despite their sometimes-asymmetrical advantages, to know exactly what is the best course of action for their patients. Thus, at any particular instance in time this sense of uncertainty might be in the background, and the analyst's work demands an underlying and ongoing tolerance for the presence of this uncertainty and with it a willingness to search within one's self, to rethink positions taken and to change.

The foregoing comments about the therapist's or analyst's responsiveness and participation, as well as a tolerance for a sense of uncertainty in the therapeutic process, is an important part of the social-constructivist analytic stance. According to this perspective, the way the analyst responds influences the kind of experience that is "constructed" within the patient at that very instance. The patient's experience does not emerge in solitary isolation, but instead is in part a product of what the analyst is doing or conveying (Mitchell, 1993). According to Hoffman, in the constructivist perspective "the interaction of the experiences of the participants is constructed . . . not just in the sense of interpretation that attaches meaning to those experiences 'after the fact,' so to speak. Before that, there is the active construction of the 'fact' itself" (1998, p. 237).

According to this position, analytic therapy cannot be viewed as a standardized treatment for a medical disease, with a regimented treatment protocol; similarly it doesn't really have a set course of standard phases, with a clearly delineated beginning, middle, and end. The treatment may be an important background support for living and functioning, and in many ways the functions of the analyst or therapist may be similar to those of a parental figure, promoting change and growth through an intimate relationship that is highly valued by both participants, but which hopefully is always in the process of being outgrown.

BACKGROUND INFORMATION:
BEGINNINGS WITH SADNESS AND DESPAIR

Mark was a 13-year-old boy when he was transferred for treatment to the Orthogenic School after a brief stay at a behavior modification treatment program in California. In terms of Mark's family background, both parents are college graduates, have an upper-class income and live in a comfortable suburb north of a large midwestern city. Mark's father is a highly successful professional who owns a construction firm, and his mother has always been a homemaker. The father has been quite active and highly respected in his business dealings; however, in the marriage and within the home in general, he tended to be rather retiring and passive, usually deferring to Mark's mother. The father had been married once before and divorced; he has three adult children (ages ranging from late 30s to mid 40s) from his first marriage; all of them are college graduates and employed in the father's business. Mark's mother also had been married once before; her first husband suffered a sudden, unexpected death after only a few months of their marriage.

The mother felt that Mark's father had not really wanted a baby in their marriage and that it took considerable effort to convince him to agree with her wish to have a child. She believed that Mark was aware of his father's position that he had not wanted any more children. The mother stated that her husband had always been very frustrated with Mark's psychological condition and behaviors, having an especially difficult time with the situation because he is significantly older and not in good health. On the other hand, the mother described both herself and her husband as being overprotective of Mark. She felt that Mark may have interpreted their overprotectiveness as a sign that they felt that he was inadequate, which may have added to a sense of distance between Mark and his father.

Mark's mother felt that clearly visible school problems for Mark began as early as the fourth grade, when there was a lot of homework, and he began to spend increasingly long periods of time trying to complete it. By the beginning of sixth grade, difficulties with his homework had become more severe and were complicated by the emergence of some perfectionist tendencies. For example, he began to look up words in three different dictionaries in order finally to decide which definition to use. Eventually he began to display symptoms of an ever-deepening sense of depression, increasing physical aggression against her and her husband, obsessive symptoms, refusal to engage in basic hygiene procedures, and self-destructive gestures. He finally began to stay home from school altogether, and shortly after mid-year, he climbed onto the roof at home, threatening to jump, and was subsequently placed in a psychiatric hospital.

Returning home from that hospitalization, Mark began to engage in self-mutilating behaviors, displayed increased obsessions and rituals, and continued to be physically assaultive toward his parents, as well as extremely destructive to property in the home resulting in thousands of dollars in damage. Examples of the self-destructive behaviors included turning on a gas stove and putting his head over the burner (singing his hair in the process). In desperation, he finally began cutting himself to write notes in blood pleading for help, imploring messages that he would then leave placed around the house for his parents to find. As a result of his continuing psychological deterioration, Mark was rehospitalized at least five additional times. Finally, completely unable to function in a public school setting, he was referred to a behavior modification residential treatment center in California, which he attended briefly until his admission to the Sonia Shankman Orthogenic School at the University of Chicago.

A WORLD OF RAGEFUL COMPLAINT

I cry and I cry, and very bitterly I cry.

–Anonymous

Bitterness and Hope

I began seeing Mark in intensive analysis four times a week when he was thirteen years old, just as he was beginning to clearly enter puberty. Mark seemed to sense that there had been an emotional lack of attunement with the adults in his early life, which in turn fueled an incessant, often nearly unbearable tone of heated, aggravated complaint from him during much of the treatment. His complaints were frequently driven by an intense sense of entitlement and self-justification during his persisting angry outbursts. Over time, many staff members exposed to Mark's bitterness reacted with defensive retaliatory wishes to reject and punish him, a countertransference difficulty which others have noted in writings about working with similarly difficult young persons in residential care (Borowitz, 1970; Rinsley, 1980; Bleiberg, 1990).

Eventually, however, I was able to come to understand his ongoing and adamant complaints about other staff members, and his perception of their alleged lack of appropriate care for his needs, as a special kind of protest, reflective of a desperate hope that things could be better for him in the present, that he need not be doomed to constantly reliving the sense of emotional abandonment associated with his past. Pizer (1992) described similar observations when he noted, "As I see it, protest, like the 'antisocial gesture,' is a sign both of anger and of hope–the hope for a negotiable environment that will heed the protest as a signal of distress. Protest in the transference is the patient's act in the present to renegotiate relational failures of the past that occurred prior to the capacity for protest. The current protest is . . . both now and then" (p. 235). A similar observation was made much earlier by Winnicott, who pointed out, "The antisocial tendency implies hope. Lack of hope is the basic feature of the deprived child who, of course, is not all the time being antisocial. In the period of hope the child manifests an antisocial tendency. . . . The understanding that the antisocial act is an expression of hope is vital in the treatment of children who show the antisocial tendency. . . . Over and over again one sees the moment of hope wasted, or withered, because of . . . intolerance" (1956/1992, p. 309).

Associated with this shift in my own thinking, there were times that Mark and I were sometimes able to begin talking about the difficulties that he had in seeing that people can have differing points of view about the same or similar situations, and that the differences need not be mutually exclusive and could begin to be tolerated. At certain points in the treatment, the issue of toleration of differences involved the struggle of realizing that he was really involved in a triangle (sometimes even a *rectangle*, where the fourth point represented his rather solidified sense of the world of himself and others) of relationships with people who held their own thoughts and views, each of which may be equally real and valid with respect to his own conscious perspective (Phillips, 1997). This continuing discussion of the issue of differing viewpoints, and our attempts to understand and modify Mark's angry reactions to opinions different from his own, continued to be a major part of our work throughout the treatment. While this argumentative, oppositional stance has been viewed by some as a normal developmental process suggestive of an expectable stage of adolescent "egocentricity" or reflective of strivings for independence and autonomy, in Mark's case it was exaggerated to the point of driving him into a state of painful rejection and isolation rather than productive autonomy. It was, of course, a struggle that was made even more intense and difficult by the fact that his perceptions of inadequacies in the wider milieu treatment setting were often not grossly inaccurate.

My ability to accept and manage his continual onslaught of complaints was augmented by issues in addition to the beginning shift of my perception of his complaints as protests of hope. Mitchell (1993) has noted that within psychoanalytic theory there have been two fundamentally different approaches to hope. Within classical or traditional theories, the hope initially displayed by the patient was seen as reflective of a desire to cling to wishes for the gratification of infantile impulses, which had to be renounced in favor of a higher process of thinking more in line with the reality principle (p. 205). From this perspective, hope serves as an obstacle to therapeutic progress, where "the waiting required by hope suffocates the possibility for the spark of desire and its fulfillment. The actual object is never the right object; the time is never now. Real satisfaction is always sacrificed in the hope of eventual fulfillment at some future time" (p. 205). A contrasting view of hope, however, sees hope not as a suffocating agent, but as part of the search for a particular psychological experience wherein a genuine sense of desire may actually become possible, in which the self can begin to experience a new beginning. This contrasting tradition was imbedded in the works, for example, of Winnicott and Kohut. All of this, of course, does not address another important and sometimes discordant issue, namely the hopes of the analyst. As Mitchell (1993) observed:

> . . . The hope that the patient brings to the analysis and the hope that drives the motion of the work [including the analyst's hope] are always partially "hope for the wrong thing." The patient's initial hopes are always a complex blend of wishes and needs, hopes fashioned from pain, frustration, longing, laced with restoration, magical transformation, and retribution. According to the Greek myth, Zeus put hope in the very bottom of Pandora's box, beneath greed, vanity, slander, envy, and the other dark realms of human experience. Sometimes, hope for the right thing can be reached only through an immersion in prolonged and harrowing dread. (p. 228)

Ghent (1992) has made similar observations in his discussion of paradox as it relates to repetition and new experiences, of which the seeming opposition between hope and dread may be seen as a particular example. For example, he discussed the paradox between the urgent wish to express true need and the appearance of demanding, sometimes vengeful neediness that acts as a noisy distraction from the more genuine longings for human warmth and responsiveness. In particular, Ghent wrote, "In the course of analytic work we often find ourselves welcoming the beginning appearance of such dark forces as envy, greed, hatred, especially as they seem to be heralding the (re)vitalization of some genuine need. We may have to hold for a long period the paradoxical meaning of these intense feelings: in one moment, defensive and constrictive and, in the next, progressive and vital" (1992, pp. 142-143).

Similarly, and of more direct importance to the present case, Pizer (1992) discussed an instance of the crucial importance of the negotiation of paradox in the treatment process, where his patient was so profoundly in need of a father, but also needed to grieve the early loss of his father and the potential future that his father's presence might have allowed him to achieve. Pizer realized that he could not be his patient's father since it would be simply untrue, but also because the patient's mourning had to proceed without denial. Yet, paradoxically, it was also utterly true that for the treatment to proceed, the patient had to become, over time, "like a son to whom, in my own countertransference, I could feel like a father. I could not recognize this paradox before I had overcome my own resistance to giving . . . the guidance [my patient] requested," which was a kind of parenting that the patient had missed (p. 231). The parental feelings described by Pizer were quite similar to ones with which I had to struggle and "soul-search" in my own work with Mark. In other words, one aspect of my work with Mark could certainly be conceptualized in terms of providing him with an important "new paternal object," so desperately needed by a boy whose elderly father did not demonstrate particular feelings of care for him. This was rather clearly one of the reasons that Mark had come to feel like a psychological orphan.

The preceding illustrations lead to another factor that enabled me to meet Mark's incessant complaining protests in a more constructive manner, in particular the energizing character of what Benjamin has described as the "transference erotic" in the treatment relationship, in this case a transformation in the treatment process through which, metaphorically, the analyst begins to assume, in the patient's view, the character of the rescuing Angel (1994). For example, there were many instances when Mark's vehement criticisms of other staff members' behaviors and of his perceptions of the tenor of the general environment appeared to be a call for me to go to war on his behalf, to become his avenging Angel. It was also a desperate plea for me to validate the worth of his complaints, to confer upon him a sense of recognition and self-validation.

The issue of Mark wanting me to act as his avenging Angel, to add a sense of legitimacy to his perceptions and complaints, and to enact rectifications for him, was a difficult one for me. There were times that I was able to take action to modify aspects of the milieu, which distressed him; there were many times, however, when I had to admit that for me to act would have the greater likelihood of making things worse for him in the wider milieu setting. So to the question of whether I assumed the role of an avenging Angel, the answer would have to be "sometimes yes and sometimes not," but always struggling with a sense of ambiguity and uncertainty about whether my decision to intervene with others or not would turn out to be helpful or the opposite for him. Further, there was always the additional uncertainty about whether I could have done *more* to be helpful than I actually did at any particular time.

Enduring the Rage

The first year and a half of treatment with Mark were characterized by his almost incessant harangues of bitter complaint, protests that took a number of directions. He complained about his perception of a marked lack of understanding on the part of the dormitory counselors, especially as it related to the issue of rules. According to Mark, either the counselors didn't understand the rules of the milieu, or when told about the rules they applied them mechanically and too strictly, ignoring the individual needs of students in their care. Other complaints were directed toward supervisory staff: for example, that they didn't really understand the nature of his relationships with his parents, or that they mistook times when his parents were allied with his views about the treatment that he was receiving as examples that they were "too close" to him.

He would heatedly criticize the teaching staff members who worked with him, claiming that they were "rude," that they didn't really understand his educational needs, or that they would vainly try to motivate him by threatening to take things away from him that he truly did enjoy in the classroom. Each therapy session would be replete with such complaints, the targets of which would shift variously from classroom staff, to clinical supervisory staff, to dormitory workers, to members of the upper administration of the school. No one, it seemed, was immune from his usually scathing criticisms. From a somewhat developmental perspective, it was as though he had the *right* to complain because now he had achieved the capacity to voice the complaints he had only felt for many years, and he also had the presence of my ears to hear them. It was many months, however, before there was, on his part, some glimmer of recognition with me of the more relational quality of his complaining.

In particular, after some months of this bitterness, he came into one session and began complaining about a peer who he actually did happen to like and admire. Suddenly, he stopped the complaining, and interjected, "Maybe my bad attitude about others may actually come from me. It seems like even when I talk about good things, the bad is always in the background. Like my friendship with Joey. Even when I talk about how much I like him, in the background I can also sense that he makes me feel vulnerable, and that makes me feel like he's intimidating." At that point, the ongoing, often deafening background noise of his bitter harangues seemed to fade away for me, and I was more able to see that many of his complaints served partially as relatively successful disguises, distracting me from what was more the real point of his arguments, which were more often than not statements in the form of "I feel, therefore . . . *you are!*"

Surely, some could say, this could easily have been identified simply as a matter of projection and projective identification, even though his comments about an awareness of the connection of his "bad attitude" with his critical view of others wasn't a clear example of these mechanisms. Nevertheless, even if they were closer examples of such defensive maneuvers, it was frequently difficult to understand them so clearly as such in the sometimes-heated exchanges of our interactions in the immediate moments of the sessions. Perhaps even more important was the fact that *he* could come up with this self-observation rather than receive it from me in the form of an interpretation, which I would probably have had to preface with, "I know that you might disagree with my thought, but I wonder if your complaints about others aren't really forms of complaint about yourself." I suspect that he possibly would have received even that muted interpretation as further confirmation that I, just as the others, was against him. On the other hand, I do not propose this as a possibility either to justify the stance of analytic silence or abstinence, or to rule out the possibility that an initial rejection of such an interpretation by him might not ultimately have led to his later considering it to have some importance for him. At any rate, his ability to consider that his "bad attitudes" about others may have been related to something within himself did reflect the beginnings of a more reflective sense of super-ego or conscience as it began to emerge in the interactions between us.

Mark's own reformulation also stirred me to begin reframing some of his protests for myself, and allowed me to begin to think clearly about the things that he was possibly trying to tell me about his own feelings and to talk with him about them. The realm of feelings was one about which he later confessed he often felt somewhat out of touch, and not, he claimed, as a result of conscious suppression. For example, his complaints about other people not understanding or acting "retarded" then reminded me of a story he had told me where a second-grade teacher had once told him that he was "stupid." And again, I remembered that at another time Mark had complained that a dormitory counselor applicant acted learning disabled, and that he continued by asserting that he also was learning disabled. When I had responded that testing had indicated the contrary, he adamantly insisted, "If I *want* to say that I'm learning disabled, I *can!*" At another time, Mark and I were walking outside, and he was desperately trying to explain a complicated thought to me. Finally, in exasperation, he exclaimed, "It's so frustrating, I can only manage to say about 20% of what goes through my mind!" In other words, the fact of his very superior verbal cognitive abilities were sometimes no match for his underlying feelings of being intellectually vulnerable and somehow impaired.

I was also reminded of his complaints about people giving him things, and what he felt he had to go through in order to feel as though he had really been able to get things from others. This issue had begun with a story that he told me about his teacher, and how another student had gotten angry when the teacher was making "too deep" interpretations about the student's feelings of depression. Finally, angered by the interpretations, the other student had said to the teacher, "Why do I ever say nice things to you?" According to Mark, the teacher had responded, "Maybe so that you can take them back when you're mad at me." During the next session after he told me this anecdote, he accidentally dropped a piece of paper on the session room rug. When I reached down to pick it up, in a somewhat panicked voice he cried out, "No, don't, don't. I can do it myself. I have such a hard time letting someone do anything for me unless I've been in a big fight with them over it."

I told him that his response reminded me somewhat of the story he had told me earlier about his teacher and the other student, about the issue of conflict over giving and getting, that somehow he didn't feel that people were genuine about their gestures of giving anything to *him*, or that maybe he felt that he didn't truly deserve such gestures from others. Stated otherwise, he seemed unable to experience that people really *wanted* to give anything to him. "Yes," Mark responded, "when someone does something for me, I feel like have to argue about it, because I feel like people shouldn't give me something, or won't give me something–that I have to *win* it!"

The latter observation appeared to illustrate the very fine line that caretakers had to walk with him, i.e., that when someone did do things for him, he would become angry because the act of caretaking led him so quickly to feelings of being infantilized. Further, it involves the more general issue of whether he really *grasped* the idea of conflict, here between dependency needs versus strivings for autonomy, perhaps a universal challenge for all adolescents. I suggested that it was important for him to realize that sometimes he could be of *two* minds about things, and that his feelings of anger might well serve to hide one part of the conflict. Further, I proposed, if he somehow could manage to hold onto his awareness of the conflict that he felt, it just might temper his anger or at least make it more manageable. The next week, he came into a session and reported having started to get into a heated argument with one of his dormitory counselors. "But," he stated, "I remembered what you said, and I have been doing better about that, better able to talk about things more when I feel conflict about something."

This type of issue, of course, also involves the more existential domain of making choices and the ability to be aware that when you get something, you also lose something else. While that somewhat more abstract issue was not pursued at this point in the treatment, it did arise later in a discussion of his feelings about things that were "like him," as opposed to things with which he disagreed or felt were "not like him." We were talking about the nature of his constant complaining, and how it seemed that he had the idea that things that weren't like him were like a "false self." But, I observed to him, when we make a choice, that results in having to make some sacrifices, acts that are not necessarily wholly bad or unhealthy. In other words, we can't have *everything*, and we can't just say that the things that we have had to give up, the sacrifices involved in our making choices for other things, are essentially the "not me," that we have to hate and reject in others.

Another issue that frequently came up in our sessions involved how some of the staff members who worked with him seemed to have personalities that struck him as being extremely "rigid." By this, he referred not only to the rigidity with which they applied rules at the school, but also to the very manner in which they comported themselves in the school environment. Realizing that we were once again touching upon the expression of his own wishes for a greater sense of personal autonomy, I asked him whether he wasn't perhaps referring to how people sometimes needed to have a sense of having some external control over what happened in their daily lives. "Yes," he replied, "but they do it so much, and I get infuriated by it." "Perhaps," I responded, "it is better for us to achieve some sense of internal controls over our own behaviors, but also to realize or come to know that we really can't have *absolute* control over things, including our own fate. And maybe when *you* come to feel that way, you'll get less upset about others who can't or don't realize that such predictable control over things isn't really possible, no matter how much they try to arrange the things around them in the attempt to achieve a sense that they *do* have ultimate control over things."

At another time, as complaint after complaint continued to pile up from him in our sessions, I stated, "Now I'm going to complain about you! You go on and on about everyone else. And nothing is ever wrong about you. You don't look at yourself. Now every time that you're in here, you have to say one thoughtful thing about yourself. And you have to try to listen to *me*." Of course, in the time before the next session, I endured considerable uncertainty about whether he had taken my intervention as an attack, or whether he would be able to use it as an interaction to think about and use in a constructive manner for himself. As our next session began, he started to launch into a "list" of five complaints that he had amassed since our last meeting. I stopped him and asked, "But, any thoughts about *you*?" He responded, "I have trouble with people who . . . I feel helpless . . . and vulnerable . . . I like you very much. How do you feel about seeing me?" I responded, "I like you very much, too. And I also greatly value the time we spend together, especially your brightness and thoughtfulness, and for the things that you encourage me to think and talk about." Mark replied, "I feel great about it too, but I wish that I could meet with you even more."

This almost immediately led to an interlude, during which he spent considerable time wondering about his future, musings that were also possibly metaphoric for the treatment process in which we were deeply involved, and, at the same time, perhaps suggestive of some identification with me and the work that we were doing together. He reported, "I want to be an interior designer, one that goes for the contrasts, like creating one area that would be 'busy' and another area that would be simple, 'minimalist.' " This seemed, to me, in part a reference to wanting to build an inner life which was capable of both work and also spaces for uncomplicated, peaceful rest, in contrast to his own feelings of being unable to perform academically in the classroom and of being in constant inner turmoil. However, Mark had more direct suggestions, comments, and ideas about his conception of the treatment process, and questions about it, some of which are illustrated in the discussions which follow.

Almost at the very beginning of treatment, Mark had conveyed an interest in the process of psychotherapy when he told me that someday he wanted to work in the field of mental health. However, he stated that he didn't want to be a clinical practitioner; instead, he wanted to work in the field of mental health public policy. This position of advocacy for what he thought was appropriate treatment techniques appeared frequently during our own sessions. For example, as described earlier, he felt that I should serve in a sense as his "avenging Angel," going to war for him against the other staff members and pleading his cause to those in administrative power at the institution. "You have power," he would complain, "so why don't you fight more? You just stay off to the side doing your therapy thing." At another time, he asserted that all of the problems in the classrooms and the dormitories existed because I didn't spend more of my time teaching and communicating with the staff.

On the other hand, this was quite a double-edged sword, since the very power he wanted me to assert led him to be fearful that I would utilize it to be in control of *him* as well. This was illustrated by his agitation over the asymmetry of the therapist/patient roles, when he complained that it was unjust that I expected him to tell me the details of the situations that he was complaining about. "That's not fair," he stated. "Why do I have to tell you everything, but you not to me. It's supposed to be equal!" I told him that I had a different perspective on this issue, that in part I was less revealing in order to be more attentive to him. "That's different than I think," he responded, "because others usually don't tell me anything about themselves or what they're thinking, because they don't want to deal with something or, even worse, they just want to be hurtful." Somewhat related to the issue of symmetry/asymmetry in roles was his growing insistence that our work together had to take the form of a more or less mutual conversation, although he was adamant that I had to learn how to tailor my part in the conversation so that it didn't feel like an interruption to his train of thought. Otherwise, he feared, he wouldn't reach the proper conclusion that he was trying to convey to me.

At another time, Mark and I got into an extended period of bickering over his tendency to subtly demand things by asking "*can* I have this or that," rather than "*may* I have it." My point in suggesting that the use of *may* was a better phrasing was that it implied more of a sense of mutuality in the request. From Mark's perspective, however, the difference in viewpoints was seen for a long time as a potential use of my power as power *over* him, to control him. On the other hand, arguments such as these were also seen as a sign of intimacy between us for him; in a sense his arguing was like wrestling with me, an active gesture of remaining engaged. At one point, he observed how much we had begun to engage in bickering with each other over our differing perspectives on things, and suddenly stated, "You're mean . . . no it's not really that, it's like we're married now. First there was the honeymoon and now the honeymoon's over." Ultimately, I had to suggest to him that in our disagreements about things, he could never admit that he might be wrong. I went on to suggest to him, "It's something like athletics. You have to try to exercise that muscle." With his curiosity aroused, he asked, "What muscle is that?" "The old 'you're right, I'm wrong' muscle," I responded. "Okay," he begrudgingly replied, "I will try harder to admit when I'm wrong. But only if I *really* think so."

His criticism of "too deep" interpretations has already been noted, and initially he was quite skeptical about the usefulness of genetic interpretations about the past. Early in our work together, Mark and his parents had attempted outside supplemental family therapy. Mark would return from those sessions quite pessimistic about whether they were really worthwhile; his major complaint was that they tended to focus on the past and that didn't really resolve anything, only seeming to stir his parents up against him. He stated that he felt like therapy was much more useful when it focused on the present, on what was going on in the "here and now." Somewhat later in our work, he began to modify this view, speculating that people who were rude (like him) probably had bad childhoods or bad experiences with their parents when they were young. Many months later, he came to assert that probably 95% of the past is irrelevant, but that 5% must be important and have *something* to do with how we are.

It was only at this point that he began to be more reflective about the possibility that part of the reasons he disliked certain persons in his present environment had something to do with things he had experienced in the past, or irritations that he harbored about his own parents' treatment of him while he was a child. At the time of the conclusion of this series of vignettes describing the still ongoing treatment process with this young adolescent boy, Mark had made considerable progress in being able to establish a more positive relationship with his family, and in therapy he had become noticeably more reflective about the mediation about the reciprocal effects between the self, particularly himself, and the external environment. Further, he was beginning to be more thoughtful about his feelings of ambivalence; for example, in discussing very conflictual difficulties that he was experiencing in trying to manage his feelings in a relationship with a particular staff person, he observed, "It isn't hard to hate bad people, but it's very painful to have angry wishes to reject people that you really care about."

CONCLUSION

This paper has discussed certain aspects of the analytic process that emerged in work with an adolescent boy who, for lack of better diagnostic specificity, had come to feel as though he was a psychological orphan. The analytic process described in this short report ranged from comments about the boy's incessant protest and complaints, his ongoing expressions of rage, his feelings of hope and dread in an intimate relationship (Mitchell, 1993), our mutual feelings of affection, and aspects of conducting analytic work within a residential therapeutic environment experienced by the boy as non-responsive to his needs.

The discussion described certain aspects of the relational perspective in the treatment of this young boy. In discussing the actual process material, the paper described how viewing his rageful outbursts in the treatment sessions as a special protest of desperate hope, with an optimistic view of the boy's psychic future, facilitated the maintenance of a perspective which enabled me to view the targets of his rage as partly intensified reflections of his own despairing feelings of vulnerability and helplessness. The latter included his strong conviction that he was learning disabled, feelings of being unable to experience that other people really had any genuine desire to give him anything, his relative inability to really grasp and contain the idea of psychic conflict, and a lack of understanding that others' perspectives could be of any use for him, or even just *might* be more valid than his own.

The treatment dialogue often focused reflexively back upon the analytic process itself, with many discussions of the process of treatment, the issue of discussion and interpretation versus enactment and doing in the actual wider treatment milieu, symmetry/asymmetry in therapist/patient roles, the enhancement of a sense of mutuality in our relationship, and the value for him of work in the here-and-now versus deep interpretations. The treatment also illustrated the importance, for this boy, of my accepting his tender feelings of attachment for me, as well as his need for me to acknowledge my own feelings of affection for him. Further, there was reference to his need for me to acknowledge his wishes for me to act as his "saving angel" in the wider residential environment, although it was not always possible for me to actually intervene in that manner on his behalf. The presentation concluded with some brief comments about the beginning steps of progress that were made by this adolescent boy in his attempts to reach out and establish relationships with others, as painful as that might be for him.

REFERENCES

Altman, N. (1994). A perspective on child psychoanalysis 1994: The recognition of relational theory and technique in child treatment. *Psychoanalytic Psychology, 11* (3), 383-395.

Altman, N. (1995). *The Analyst in the Inner City.* Hillsdale NJ and London: The Analytic Press.

Benjamin, J. A. (1994). What angel would hear me? The erotics of transference. *Psychoanalytic Inquiry, 14* (4), 535-557.

Benjamin, J. A. (1995). *Like Subjects, Love Objects.* New Haven, CT: Yale University Press.

Blos, P. (1962). *On Adolescence: A Psychoanalytic Perspective.* New York: Free Press.

Blos, P. (1979). *The Adolescent Passage.* New York: International Universities Press, Inc.

Bollas, C. (1987). *The Shadow of the Object. Psychoanalysis of the Unknown Thought.* New York: Columbia University Press.

Borowitz, G. H. (1970). The therapeutic utilization of emotions and attitudes evoked in the caretakers of disturbed children. *British Journal of Medical Psychology, 43,* 129-139.

Bullard, D. M. (1990). Reflections on the hospital treatment of adolescents at Chestnut Lodge. *Adolescent Psychiatry, 18,* 305-321.

Colm, H. (1966). *The Existentialist Approach to Psychotherapy with Adults and Children.* New York: Grune & Stratton.

Ehrenberg, D. B. (1992). *The Intimate Edge. Extending the Reach of Psychoanalytic Interaction.* New York/London: Norton.

Ekstein, R., Wallerstein, J. S., & Mandelbaum, A. (1992). Countertransference in the residential treatment of children. In J. R. Brandell (Ed.), *Countertransference in*

Psychotherapy with Children and Adolescents. Northvale, NJ: Jason Aronson, Inc., pp. 59-87.

Erikson, E. (1958). *Childhood and Society.* New York: W. W. Norton & Co.

Erikson, E. (1959). *Identity and the Life Cycle.* (Psychological Issues Monograph 1). New York: International Universities Press.

Erikson, E. (1968). *Identity: Youth and Crisis.* New York: W. W. Norton & Co.

Fairbairn, W. R. D. (1952). *An Object-Relations Theory of the Personality.* New York: Basic Books.

Ferenczi, S. (1913/1952) The little chanticleer. In *First Contributions to Psychoanalysis.* (Trans. E. Jones). London: Hogarth Press, 240-252.

Ferenczi, S. (1931/1955). Child analysis in the analysis of adults. In Michael Baling (Ed.), *Final Contributions to the Problems and Methods of Psychoanalysis.* New York: Basic Books.

Fonagy, P., & Target, M. (1998). Mentalization and the changing aims of child analysis. *Psychoanalytic Dialogues, 8* (1), 87-114.

Frankel, J. B. (1998). The play's the thing: How the essential processes of therapy are seen most clearly in child therapy. *Psychoanalytic Dialogues, 8* (1), 149-182.

Freud, A. (1958). Adolescence. *Psychoanalytic Study of the Child, 13,* 255-278.

Freud, S. (1905/1962). *Three Contributions to the Theory of Sex.* New York: E. P. Dutton & Co.

Ghent, E. (1992). Paradox and process. *Psychoanalytic Dialogues, 2* (2), 135-159.

Ghent, E. (1995). Interaction in the psychoanalytic situation. *Psychoanalytic Dialogues, 5* (3), 479-491.

Gill, M. M. (1982). *Analysis of Transference, Vol. I: Theory and Technique.* New York: International Universities Press.

Gill, M. M. (1994). *Psychoanalysis in Transition.* Hillsdale, NJ: The Analytic Press.

Green, M. R. (1972). The interpersonal approach to child therapy. In Benjamin B. Wolman (Ed.), *Handbook of Child Psychoanalysis: Research, Theory and Practice.* New York: Van Nostrand Reinhold Company, pp. 514-566.

Hoffman, I. Z. (1987). The value of uncertainty in psychoanalytic practice. *Contemporary Psychoanalysis, 23* (2), 205-215.

Hoffman, I. Z. (1992). Expressive participation and psychoanalytic discipline. *Contemporary Psychoanalysis, 28* (1), 1-15.

Hoffman, I. Z. (1994). Dialectical thinking and therapeutic action in the psychoanalytic process. *Psychoanalytic Quarterly, 63,* 187-218.

Hoffman, I. Z. (1998). *Ritual and Spontaneity in the Psychoanalytic Process.* Hillsdale, NJ and London: The Analytic Press.

Jacobson, E. (1954). The self and the object world. *Psychoanalytic Study of the Child, 9,* 75-127.

Jacobson, E. (1961). Adolescent moods and the remodeling of psychic structures in adolescence. *Psychoanalytic Study of the Child, 16,* 164-183.

Jacobson, E. (1964). *The Self and the Object World.* New York: International Universities Press.

Jones, E. (1922/1948). Some problems of adolescence. *Papers on Psychoanalysis.* London: Bailliere, Tindall & Co., pp. 389-406.

Klein, M. (1932). *The Psycho-Analysis of Children.* London: Hogarth Press.

Klein, M. (1959/1984). Our adult world and its roots in infancy. In *Envy and Gratitude and Other Works: 1946-1963.* New York: Free Press, pp. 247-263.

Kohut, H. (1971). *The Analysis of the Self.* New York: International Universities Press.

Kohut, H. (1972) Thoughts on narcissism and narcissistic rage. *Psychoanalytic Study of the Child, 27,* 360-400.

Kohut, H. (1977). *The Restoration of the Self.* New York: International Universities Press.

Levenson, E. (1983). *The Ambiguity of Change. An Inquiry into the Nature of Psychoanalytic Reality.* New York: Basic Books.

Mahler, M. S. (1952). On child psychosis and schizophrenia: Autistic and symbiotic infantile psychoses. *Psychoanalytic Study of the Child, 7,* 286-305.

Mahler, M. S. (1971). A study of the separation-individuation process and its possible application to borderline phenomena in the psychoanalytic situation. *Psychoanalytic Study of the Child, 26,* 403-424.

Mahler, M. S. (1972). Rapproachment subphase of separation-individuation process. *Psychoanalytic Quarterly, 41,* 487-506.

Mahler, M. S. (1975). On the current status of the infantile neurosis. *Journal of the American Psychoanalytic Association, 23,* 327-333.

Mahler, M. S., & Furer, M. (1968). *On Human Symbiosis and the Vicissitudes of Individuation.* New York: International Universities Press.

Mitchell, S. A. (1993). *Hope and Dread in the Psychoanalysis.* New York: Basic Books.

Mitchell, S. A. (1997). *Influence and Autonomy in Psychoanalysis.* Hillsdale, NJ and London: The Analytic Press.

Modell, A. H. (1990). *Other Times, Other Realities: Toward a Theory of Psychoanalytic Treatment.* Cambridge, MA: Harvard University Press.

Phillips, A. (1997). Making it new enough. Commentary on paper by Altman. *Psychoanalytic Dialogues, 7* (6), 741-752.

Piaget, J. The intellectual development of the adolescent. In A. H. Esman (Ed.), *The Psychology of Adolescence.* New York: International Universities Press, pp. 104-108.

Pizer, S. A. (1992). The negotiation of paradox in the analytic process. *Psychoanalytic Dialogues, 2* (2), 215-240.

Racker, H. (1968). *Transference and Countertransference.* Madison, CT: International Universities Press.

Redl, F., & Wineman, D. (1951). *Children Who Hate.* Glencoe, IL: The Free Press.

Redl, F., & Wineman, D. (1952). *Controls from Within.* Glencoe, IL: The Free Press.

Rinsley, D. B. (1974). Special education for adolescents in residential psychiatric treatment. *Adolescent Psychiatry, 3,* 394-418.

Rinsley, D. B. (1980). *Treatment of the Severely Disturbed Adolescent.* New York and London: Jason Aronson.

Searles, H. F. (1965). *Collected Papers on Schizophrenia and Related Subjects.* New York: International Universities Press.

Stern, D. (1997). *Unformulated Experience: From Dissociation to Imagination in Psychoanalysis.* Hillsdale, NJ and London: The Analytic Press.

Stolorow, R. D., & Atwood, G. E. (1997). *Contexts of Being: The Intersubjective Foundations of Psychological Life*. Hillsdale, NJ: The Analytic Press.

Winnicott, D. W. (1956/1992). The antisocial tendency. In D. W. Winnicott, *Through Paediatrics to Psycho-Analysis: Collected Papers*. New York: Brunner/Mazel.

Winnicott, D. W. (1958). *Through Paediatrics to Psychoanalysis*. London: Hogarth.

Winnicott, D. W. (1971). *The Maturational Process and the Facilitating Environment*. New York: International Universities Press.

Wolf, E. S. (1980) Tomorrow's self: Heinz Kohut's contribution to adolescent psychiatry. *Adolescent Psychiatry, 5*, 41-50.

Zimmerman, D. P. (1990). Notes on the history of adolescent inpatient and residential treatment. *Adolescence, 25* (97), 9-38.

BIOGRAPHICAL NOTE

D. Patrick Zimmerman, PsyD, is Assistant Director, Admissions and Psychotherapy Services, The Sonia Shankman Orthogenic School. He is also Lecturer, The Department of Psychiatry and The Committee on Human Development, The University of Chicago. In addition, he serves as a member of the Senior Associate Core Faculty at the Illinois School of Professional Psychology/Chicago. He is a graduate of the Chicago Center for Psychoanalysis and a member of the CCP Board of Directors.

Parallel Dimensions in Child, Adolescent, and Adult Analytic Work

D. Patrick Zimmerman, PsyD

SUMMARY. This paper begins with the proposal that there are certain essential processes of therapy, including play as the renegotiation of self-other relationships that are fully present in work with children. This leads to a discussion of historical material about the use of play in analytic work with children, associated with the emergence of ideas about the analytic work with children as a "less pure" form of analysis. The paper then presents a theoretical discussion of play as a continuous and basic function in psychoanalysis, where play is seen as a way of engagement, which includes both the negotiation of paradox and the capacity for the use of metaphor in treatment. This is associated with a brief dis-

The author may be written at: The Sonia Shankman Orthogenic School, The University of Chicago, 1365 East 60th Street, Chicago, IL 60637 (E-mail: pzimmerm@midway.uchicago.edu).

A version of this paper was presented at the 110th Annual Meeting of the American Psychological Association, August 23rd, 2002, Chicago, Illinois. A version of this paper appeared in *Therapeutic Communities* (2002), *23* (3), 191-205. Some anecdotal material appeared in "The Little Turtle's Progress: A Reconsideration of the Short versus Long-Term Residential Treatment Controversy," *Children and Youth Services Review*, *15* (3), 219-243, 1993 (Copyright © 1993, adapted with permission from Elsevier Science). Other anecdotal material appeared in "Desperation and Hope in the Analysis of a 'Thrown-Away' Adolescent Boy," *Psychoanalytic Psychology*, *16* (2), 198-232, 1999 (Copyright © 1999 by the Educational Publishing Foundation. Adapted with permission).

[Haworth co-indexing entry note]: "Parallel Dimensions in Child, Adolescent, and Adult Analytic Work." Zimmerman, D. Patrick. Co-published simultaneously in *Residential Treatment for Children & Youth* (The Haworth Press, Inc.) Vol. 20, No. 4, 2003, pp. 25-41; and: *Psychotherapy in Group Care: Making Life Good Enough* (ed: D. Patrick Zimmerman et al.) The Haworth Press, Inc., 2003, pp. 25-41. Single or multiple copies of this article are available for a fee from The Haworth Document Delivery Service [1-800-HAWORTH, 9:00 a.m. - 5:00 p.m. (EST). E-mail address: docdelivery@haworthpress.com].

http://www.haworthpress.com/store/product.asp?sku=J007

10.1300/J007v20n04_02

cussion of play as non-linear versus non-play as linear, reflected in more general theories about essentialist versus more relational, constructivist approaches to treatment. Vignettes from analytic work conducted with two young persons in residential care then illustrate how play can function as an essential process of therapy. *[Article copies available for a fee from The Haworth Document Delivery Service: 1-800-HAWORTH. E-mail address: <docdelivery@haworthpress.com> Website: <http://www.HaworthPress.com> © 2003 by The Haworth Press, Inc. All rights reserved.]*

KEYWORDS. Play, child psychotherapy, adolescent psychotherapy, relational psychotherapy, residential treatment, Melanie Klein, Anna Freud

INTRODUCTION

In Jay Frankel's engaging (1998) article on child therapy, I was pleased to read his direct assertion that there are certain essential processes of therapy, such as play as a critical function in the therapeutic renegotiations of self-other relationships, which are fully present in work with young persons. While today few clinicians would think that play is not an essential technique promoting the transformation of self-other relations in analytic work in children, this has not always been the case. Frankel reminds us that for many years, child therapy (and, I might add, adolescent therapy) was held to be a less than optimal modification of adult therapy. There is in fact a historical theoretical background, associated with the issue of play in analytic work, which contributed to the assumption that child analysis is a "less pure" form of analytic treatment.

HISTORICAL ISSUES IN CHILD AND ADULT ANALYTIC WORK

Seventy years ago, Melanie Klein (1932) outlined her differences from the classical Freudian position, which included her beliefs that children are quite capable of producing a transference neurosis, that the technique of play analysis was an equivalent of the technique of adult analysis, and that full analytic results could be obtained by interpreting soon, deeply and in the smallest detail. Accordingly, she was convinced, the child brings as many associations to the separate elements of play as adults do to the separate elements of their dreams. Moreover, she argued that the talking that a child does during play could be understood to have the same characteristics of adult free associations.

Anna Freud strongly disagreed with Melanie Klein's positions in her own presentations on the psychoanalytic treatment of children (1946/1964). For her, child analysis required a preparatory period not necessary for adults, and there was little justification for equating a child's play activity with the adult's free associations. Regarding the latter, she stated that "[If] the child's play is not dominated by the same purposive attitude as the adult's free association, there is no justification for treating it as having the same significance. Instead of being invested with symbolic meaning it may sometimes admit of a harmless explanation" (1946/1964, p. 35). Further, according to Anna Freud, the child was unable to form a transference-neurosis, since his/her original objects are still real and present as love objects–not only in fantasy as with the adult neurotic (1946/1964, p. 40). In addition, Ms. Freud also disparaged Melanie Klein's technique of making early interpretations to the depths of the unconscious, and then to the ego, which contradicted her own position that work must be done first at the surface, working through the resistances and distortions of the preconscious and conscious before reaching down to the deeper layers of the child's mind (1946/1964, p. 85).

According to Anna Freud, in "true" analysis, e.g., the analysis of adults, we remain "impersonal and shadowy, a blank page on which the patient can inscribe his transference fantasies. . . . We avoid either issuing prohibitions or allowing gratifications" (1946/1964, p. 41). In this manner, when the patient forms an impression of the analyst, "it is easy to make clear to him that he has brought the material for this impression from his own past" (p. 41). On the other hand, according to Ms. Freud, the child analyst suffers from the impossibility of being a shadowy, blank page, empty screen to the child. In addition, the child analyst cannot rely solely upon interpretations; instead the analytic work must extend to the provision of educative functions, which unfortunately tend to efface the clarity of transference and the possibility of the emergence of the "true" transference neurosis characteristic of the more formal analysis of adults (p. 42).

From one point of view, the disputes between Melanie Klein and Anna Freud rested upon different perspectives regarding a similarly traditional assumption about adult analysis. Both presumed that an essential feature of adult analysis, which in a sense made it analysis "proper," was the focus upon a line of continuity that leads from the present to the past, a linear perspective of treatment, which in turn facilitates historical insight as the mutative factor in analysis. Melanie Klein assumed that for children the interpretation of children's play could provide access to that same linear line of continuity, whereas Anna Freud felt that this assumption was an unwarranted extension of the usefulness of play in clinical work.

In the United States, it was Sigmund Freud's drive theory and Anna Freud's contributions to ego psychology that prevailed, along with Anna Freud's view of child analytic work. The views of the adherents of this classical perspective became quite influential, and as a consequence child work came to be viewed by many as a diluted form of analytic technique. As recently as 1999 Abrams presented an essay as an attempt to provide a conciliatory exchange between two analysts, one an adult classical clinician, the other principally recognized for her work with children. The position of the adult analyst proposed that the essential feature of analysis proper was the focus upon the line of continuity that leads from the present back to the past, and ultimately to insight about the past, a sense of linearity that was portrayed as "both clinically useful and a distinguished form of scientific thinking" (p. 5). Child analysis, on the other hand, was characterized as a more forward engagement with the often-unexpected construction of potentially new, but essentially discontinuous mental organizations. While Abrams speaks of these as "differences," there remains the underlying notion that child work deviates from and is a less optimal clinical procedure than the more formal model of adult analysis.

PLAY VERSUS NON-PLAY

When one adopts a perspective about the therapeutic treatment process as non-linear, where past and present, or continuity and discontinuity, co-exist in a changing figure-ground relationship, then the capacity for and activity of play as a crucial and similar dimension of treatment for both children and adults emerges once again. Nevertheless, the proposition that play is an essential process of therapy in general calls forth certain important issues, foremost among which might be: what is play versus what is non-play? One way of thinking about this question might be to suggest that play involves making choices where there is an element of arbitrariness in those choices. In that sense, play is non-linear, takes different forms, and is constructivist in the play space that some have called the "Third," or the "sense" of the analytic experience. Non-play, conversely, is linear and aims for *one* meaning. As contrasted with play as non-linear and constructivist, non-play may be viewed as linear and *essentialist*. Seen in this light, play involves choosing one thing over another, but not simply choosing because one choice is intrinsically better. The *sense of arbitrariness* about it is what makes it play. It is *a* way of engagement that is invented, an engagement that is not *the* way to be, but rather a way to be. Further, the element of arbitrariness of this sense of play doesn't detract from one's investment in it, for one *can* at the same time be quite serious about it.

When play is considered in this manner, some authors have noted the relationship between both the negotiation of paradox and the use of metaphor to the capacity for play in treatment. This relationship is perhaps more applicable or clearly reflected in the play of adolescents and adults than in that of younger children, although there may well be many times when paradox and metaphor are qualities that can be detected in children's play as well. Nevertheless, I do think that there are essential differences between the responses to these elements of play in the treatment of younger persons, versus work with adults. Among those differences, I would suggest that *a mutual sense of recognition* of the metaphoric meanings within this dimension in work with children and adolescents is perhaps more important than the manifest interpretive work with which one might engage regarding elements of play in treatment with adults.

Nevertheless, aside from the qualifications just mentioned, the relationship between paradox, metaphor, and play is seldom made explicit. One might say that the relationship of play to paradox might be conceived as nested within a sense of *entertainment*, or more specifically upon the capacity to *entertain* the possibility that two contradictory things co-exist. Similarly, the relationship of play to metaphor rests upon the capacity to harbor an appreciation that the metaphor conveys symbolic meaning. For example, with regard to the latter, stories told in treatment may often be characterized as the unconscious use of metaphor. Interpretation, then, can be viewed as a technique for making the metaphor conscious. In this sense, interpretation is not an essentialist reflection of the nature of reality. Rather, it is an invitation for the patient to think about the interpretation, and about how he or she might want to feel, react, or behave in different ways. A metaphor has symbolic meaning, but it might well have a *number* of symbolic meanings (and to both the patient and analyst). Similarly, since it might have a number of meanings, the analyst's choice of interpretations reflects a choice among other possible interpretations.

FROM OBJECTIVISM TO CONSTRUCTIVISM

The distinction between play as non-linear and constructivist, versus non-play as linear and essentialist, reflects more general theoretical issues related to analytic theory and technique. It is beyond the scope of this paper to discuss in substantial detail the issues involved in the constructivist versus essentialist or objectivist positions, but they have been examined in substantial depth elsewhere (Gill, 1994; Hoffman, 1998; Lear, 1998, pp. 16-32; Zimmerman, 1999, 2000). In general, what I understand as the essentialist, positivist, or objectivist model of treatment is a view of the process in which the analyst or therapist is thought to be capable of maintaining a stance outside the interaction with the patient. From this stand outside the interaction, it is believed that the worker can then generate rather self-assured judgments about the patient's history, dynamics, and transference and about what they should do from moment to moment (Hoffman, 1998, p. 164).

In this view, the analyst or therapist applies what he or she "knows" on the basis of a particular theory in a systematic manner to achieve certain immediate, long-standing results, an approach that is implicitly diagnostic and prescriptive (Hoffman, 1998, pp. 164-165). In other words, having assessed the nature of the patient's emotional disturbance, the worker implements a prescribed approach of specific interventions derived from one or another theoretical framework. Generally, then, a central feature of the positivist, essentialist, or objectivist view is the assumption that clinical workers, as a consequence of their acquired body of knowledge about particular theories and associated techniques, can be quite self-confident, not only about their sense of what their patients are doing and experiencing, but also about the nature of their own engagement or interventions at any particular moment.

In the constructivist view of treatment, the patient's experience is not viewed as reflective of the relatively "hard facts" of his or her history and dynamics. From this perspective, the patient's experience is assumed to be more ambiguous and pliable. Interpretations, then, are seen as *suggestions* of ways that the patient's experience might be organized among a wide range of possible ways that might be possible. This stance also challenges the idea that analytic workers can know the personal meaning of their own actions on an ongoing basis in the treatment process, both in a retrospective and prospective manner. The objectivist or essentialist view proposes that the analytic worker can confidently assume the position of a relatively detached listener, since that stance alone facilitates the emergence of transference, the development of insight, and the consequential promotion of possibilities for new experiences.

From the constructivist position, while an appreciation of the potential value of a relatively detached stance is not dismissed, there is also a sense of uncertainty about its meaning to oneself and to the patient at any particular moment, along with the acknowledgement that other kinds of interaction might be possible and valuable. Working within this perspective confronts the analytic worker with a new sense of personal responsibility regarding whatever he or she chooses to do from moment to moment. In this model, there is a dialectical movement between the personal and the technical; neither exists in a pure form, isolated from the other (Hoffman, 1998, p. 167). While the analyst working in the constructivist model makes no claims to a transcendence of their own subjectivity, nor to the objective kinds of knowledge that an objectivist or essentialist model might offer, this does not mean that the worker does not make use of acquired knowledge from a number of sources, including personal life experiences, common sense, clinical experiences, and a grasp of various theories. However, particular theories are freed from their positivist anchors and adapted to suit the analytic worker with a particular patient at a specific moment.

In sum, one way of describing the essential, practical potential of the shift from an essentialist to a constructivist model is to maintain that while conviction based on objective knowledge is decreased, self-assurance based upon the worker's subjective experience is increased (Hoffman, 1998, p. 168; Mitchell, 1991, p. 153). Ideally, a new kind of openness accompanies this shift, along with an awareness of a new kind of uncertainty. One embraces this sense of uncertainty as a valuable appreciation of the fact that the analytic worker is always in a position of some uncertainty as to the nature of what has emerged in the patient and him or herself as sources for action. It is an acknowledgement of a kind of uncertainty that is quite different from the objectivist's concern about whether a particular intervention is the "correct" one or not. Rather, it is an uncertainty that has to do with the analytic worker's sense that the kind of experiential world that he or she creates with the patient is selected at the expense of many other possibilities that are unrecognized or that are unavailable to the analyst and patient for various reasons, including a range of potentially unconscious motives (Hoffman, 1998, p. 169).

PLAY AS A CONTINUOUS AND BASIC FUNCTION IN PSYCHOANALYSIS

Winnicott's well-known direct association of play with the process of psychoanalysis was summarized by his belief that "Psychotherapy has to do with two people playing with each other" (1971/1991, p. 38). Embedded in this claim was the conviction that play in the therapeutic situation provides for an expansion of boundaries, leading to a sudden sense of enjoyment associated with the pleasure of experiencing an unanticipated freedom of exploration. More recently, Parsons (1999) has again emphasized that play contributes to the analytic treatment as a continuous underlying function. While his discussion ranges from the play of children to that of adults, some might argue that his positions are more clearly manifested in the play of adolescents and adults. In his discussion, Parsons argues that play is a current which enables us "to sustain a paradoxical reality . . . [a] paradox [which] is the framework of psychoanalysis" (p. 871). Play, then, is involved with paradox, and paradox denotes ways of thinking or acting which have to be accepted as real, but that acceptance is only possible if we know that they're not real. Play contains and sustains paradox, and at the same time it resonates with the capacity for metaphor.

In other words, play becomes possible when organisms no longer respond solely on the basis of another's behavior, but are able to think, communicate about, and even transform the meaning of the behavior and its content. In play, then, the paradoxical and metaphoric infuse the actions in which we engage; in this realm, the actions in which we engage do not simply denote what those actions *for which they stand* would appear to convey. Examples of this, provided by Parsons, include Karate training (playful, even though appearing serious and "tough") or the playful nips of dogs at play with each other.

In terms of psychotherapy, according to Parsons, paradox involves a number of issues, including, at a more general level, the fact that what happens within the treatment session is to be considered differently from what happens outside it. Paradox as the essential basis of play is also part of the experience of transference, in that it can be understood to be both real and not real. Other examples of play and paradox in treatment include the experience of hope versus the fear of losing what we do already know as familiar, the simultaneous experience of wanting versus not-wanting, and the expression of hate as a simultaneous expression of love. Parsons concludes, "Play in the analytic relationship takes place by the evolution of shared experience in an intermediate space, where patient and analyst have the possibility of finding, by a mixed process of invention and discovery, new ways of knowing and of being known that their starting-point gave no means of predicting" (1999, p. 883).

PLAY, PARADOX, AND METAPHOR

Ghent (1992) and Pizer (1992) have focused more particularly upon the issues of paradox and metaphor as fundamental aspects of play in the therapeutic relationship, perhaps more clearly visible in work with adolescents and adults. However, Altman (1997) recently presented case material that vividly illustrates importance of recognizing the metaphoric background of play as an ideal therapeutic modality in his work with a seven-year-old boy. Ghent (1992) defined paradox as the recognition and acceptance of the coexistence of two disparate and contradictory kinds of experience. According to Ghent, an important element of therapeutic technique is to help the patient cope with the implicit paradoxes of the treatment relationship. Among these are the interplay of different levels of reality; intimacy experienced as real in the treatment relationship versus that intimacy serving as a "proxy" for that to be achieved in ordinary life; the treatment relationship as being both one of equality, yet also by nature an asymmetric one; the phenomena of transference and countertransference as reflecting both issues related to ordinary life, as well as those deriving from the therapeutic frame; and the paradoxical issue of gratification, in that there are times when it is neither fulfilled, but also not suppressed. Ghent (1992) proposed, somewhat poetically, that the route to "truth" is a passage through the intensity of illusions, and that analysis is the *playpen* for transference and countertransference, both of which are seen as metaphoric efforts of "knocking on the walls of illusions" (p. 138).

In Ghent's view, additional forms of paradox, often seen as polarities, include: expressions of "neediness" versus true need; malignant regression versus benign regression; object destruction versus object discovery; and possessiveness as an expression of greed versus a striving for autonomy. While there are times that the benign aspect of each of these paradoxes can be more easily discerned, this is often not the case. And it is in the instances of the latter that one needs the integrative function of being able to hold onto the *tension* of paradox in general, the capacity to appreciate multiple perspectives without having to arrive at a resolution when no true resolution is either immediately foreseeable or ultimately possible.

For Pizer (1992), the negotiation of play as paradox in treatment involves the negotiation of meaning between analyst and patient and the development of mutually useful metaphors, which in turn can be described as the exchange of "Winnicottian" squiggles between the analyst and patient. More particular examples of the presence and operation of the paradoxical process in treatment, according to Pizer, include (1) the concept of the emergent self as involved with both the care one receives and the care that one is able to give; (2) instances of transference where, in a successful treatment, we cannot *be* the actual object of transference, but we have *to be like*, even *feel like* the original object; and (3) signs of protest seen either as an antisocial gesture or as an expression of hope, the survival of a wish that things can be better (pp. 221, 223, 235). In general, Pizer sees the process of negotiation of paradox in the treatment setting as a kind of duet, in one sense the two participants involved in a kind of ongoing mutual, lyrical play.

PLAY IN ANALYTIC WORK WITH CHILDREN AND ADOLESCENTS

In line with Frankel's position about play as an essential process of both child and adult treatment, my discussion now turns to a consideration of both the physical and verbal elements of play which were important processes of communication and growth in the analytic treatment of two young persons who were students in longer-term residential care at the Sonia Shankman

Orthogenic School at the University of Chicago. The Orthogenic School is located on the university campus in an urban residential neighborhood (Bettelheim, 1950, 1955, 1974; Zimmerman & Cohler, 1998). The school is coeducational and presently serves over 40 children and adolescents. Through the 1980s, the average length of residency was over 5 years, although in recent times the length of stay has decreased somewhat. With rare exceptions, students' emotional disturbances have been of fairly early origin and refractory to previous treatment interventions. The school provides a structured milieu setting, with an emphasis on an interdisciplinary treatment staff that provides individual and group psychotherapy, psychopharmacological treatment, accredited special education school services, and therapeutic arts and recreation programming.

The vignettes presented from both cases illustrate, I think, how I have described play as non-linear, taking different forms, and constructivist in the play space that some have called the "Third," or the "sense" of the analytic experience. However, the presentation of play experiences in these two vignettes does raise a very important question, i.e., when is play to be considered as "literal" play versus "metaphorical" play? From my perspective, this question represents a more general tendency for our concepts in psychoanalysis to reflect a dichotomous form of thinking: fantasy versus reality, repetition versus new experience, self-expression versus responsiveness to others, technique versus personal relationship, interpretation versus action and enactment, construction versus discovery (Hoffman, 1998, p. 200). While there is a sense that these polarities may often appear as rather clearly differentiated from each other, the challenge for the dialectical constructivist is not only to recognize their differences, but also to find the effects of each polarity upon the other, and even to recognize aspects of each pole that are represented within the other. In this sense, then, I would consider that what appears to be "literal" play in the foreground reflects a sense of "metaphoric" play in the background. Therefore, as an alternative to viewing literal versus metaphorical play in a dichotomous manner, one might view each mode of play as influencing, interpenetrating the other.

Finally, there are some who might be critical of what appears to be a lack of discussion about a more clear engagement in these vignettes with particular developmental issues regarding young people. While this is indeed a crucial dimension of work with children and adolescents, I should somewhat clarify my own perspective on this aspect of analytic work with young persons. In my work with children and adolescents, I have found that particular theories of motivation and development are indeed valuable in helping to identify or formulate various interactions and experiences which come to the foreground at different times in the treatment process. Nevertheless, while theorists have differed with regard to the developmental issues or tasks that they believe are the most important to be mastered, I do not feel compelled to favor a particular theory in order to benefit from the specific account of development that each theorist considers pivotal or fundamental. In this sense, I tend to agree with Irwin Hoffman's (1987) position that the more openness that there is to various theoretical developmental perspectives and languages, the more likely it might be that what the young person and the analyst may resist in formulating at one moment may well be more clearly articulated at a later time (p. 211).

The Little Turtle Speaks

Timmy was a seven-year-old boy referred for residential treatment due to his uncontrollable rages which resulted in self-destructive behaviors and attempts to do serious physical harm to a younger sister. Perhaps associated with this, the temperamental match between Timmy and his mother had been a difficult one; the mother was easily agitated, while Timmy was himself highly excitable due to what appeared to be a lack of effective stimulus barriers between himself and the outside world. In the residential setting, he provoked ongoing peer conflicts in his dormitory, became emotionally explosive in both the dormitory and classroom, and seemingly minor and subtle precipitants would quickly escalate to the expression of massive verbal and physical rage upon many staff persons who worked with him.

In sharp distinction to the increasingly rageful behavior he had come to display in the general school environment, during the first few weeks of individual therapy Timmy would come to therapy and spend almost the whole session sitting stiffly and statue-like on the couch across from me, trying desperately to think of something to say. His attempts to talk would usually trail off with his murmuring, "I don't know what to say . . . I forget everything I could say." This ongoing seemingly massively repressed, amnesiac-like state would leave him appearing to feel profoundly distressed and depressed. Even though he knew there were toys in the room, with which he could play or even just use to distract himself from his extreme discomfort, he would persist in sitting and desperately trying to find a way to relate to me by talking. For many weeks, no form of reassurance that I would consider anything that he might be able to say to be valuable in his session facilitated his being able to talk or ameliorated his feelings of failure and depression in the face of this amnesiac-like state.

I eventually came to sense that my own growing feelings of frustration may have been a reflection of the kind of frustration that he may have experienced in trying to establish emotional contact with his mother during his early years. Second, I began to understand his own feelings of failure and depression in those sessions as possibly reflective of his own reactions to long-standing feelings of emotional abandonment by his mother (and fears of abandonment by his family related to the real precipitants of his hospitalization and subsequent residential placement). He was eventually able to tell me that he was terrified that because he wasn't able to talk, he wasn't "good enough" for sessions and, therefore, I probably didn't want him in therapy and wanted to get rid of him. In a sense, then, the silences also came to suggest the possible direction of the unfolding of his transference feelings to me in the treatment process, namely to some extent coalescing around early maternal care issues.

Finally, one day he asked me once again what he should say in the session. I replied, "Anything." Gleefully, he responded, *"Anything, anything!"* Absolutely thrilled with his joking response, he then was able to ask if I'd like for him to tell me a story. My response that I would indeed be interested in listening to his stories opened up a whole channel of creative, symbolic communications from him, which included storytelling, pretending to go to sleep and "making up" dreams, making up and singing operas in pseudo-foreign languages, and role-playing (including role-reversals, in which he would be the doctor and I would be the patient, where he asked the questions and instructed me about what responses that I, as Timmy, should give). These forms of story-telling and role-play appeared to be a way for him to free-associate, while at the same time preserving a sense of structure to protect himself against the dangers of unmanageable levels of regression or fragmentation. They also, however, enabled him to slowly begin to peek out at the world from beneath his always-precarious shell of repression.

Over the next few months, Timmy used these various forms of verbal play to convey to me a number of his most primitive fears and rages. For example, an early story illustrated his strong feelings of vulnerability from external threat, and also fears that the vulnerability to such danger might be contagious, when he told me a "scary" story about green, slimy, jelly-like monsters coming to get him (and probably me, too). This was succeeded in the next session by an elaboration of his strong oral needs for nurturance, which were co-mingled with rageful feelings toward his mother, through a long story about a peanut butter and jelly sandwich, out of which first came the green slimy monsters, and then his mother (from the "sticky" peanut butter side of the sandwich). When his mother jumped out, he killed her. In the following session, he continued with this theme of murderous rage at his mother, telling a story in which his mother again appeared, but in a giant crowd of green, slimy monsters. In that story, Timmy became a knight, who then slew his mother with a sword. One is tempted to view this story as an example of the paradox between object destruction versus object discovery, the expression of hate as a simultaneous wish for love, the ridding of the attacking mother as an attempt to discover the nurturant mother. Seen in this way, there is an element of the ironic in his story, which has a paradoxical effect in that it has the capacity to tame the negative while at the same time leading to an exploratory sense of excitement, along with an increase in curiosity about what might happen next.

As the months proceeded, his stories told me about his fears that no one would help him, and how he felt that it was possibly his own fault (telling me the story of the boy who cried wolf and ending it by looking down and quietly saying, "That boy in that story is me"). Periodically, then, he came to be able to tell a few simple dreams, which continued to emphasize the mixture of orality with fears of destruction, though now there came to be an element of hope: he dreamed of monsters and foxes . . . foxes eating . . . and a fox ate him, but he was finally able to escape through the fox's stomach. This sense of an emerging sense of hopefulness was also elaborated through song as he sang me his own "compositions" about the sun rising on a happier day, and another about a man pushing the alarm button on a clock and all the people in the world would "wake up."

Other stories indicated his hopefulness that the therapeutic relationship could help him deal with his feelings of fragmentation, anonymity, and lack of a true sense of self. He told me about a man named Zoo-Zoom (who, he confided, was really me), who was surrounded by thousands, millions, billions of little boys . . . all of them named Timmy T. Johnson. Zoo-Zoom had to find the real Timmy T. Johnson. He asked, "What is your name?" of boy after boy. They each responded exactly the same, "Timmy T. Johnson." Finally, one said "Timmy T. Johnson" in a very *LOW* voice. And with that, Zoo-Zoom could tell, by the very low voice, that it was the *real* Timmy T. Johnson. This story also appeared to refer to his need for me to regard him as special, in spite of the presence of even "billions" of other little boys who might even look exactly like him. The fulfillment of similar wishes for mirroring admiration from me was also apparent in the great joy and delight he took in feeling that I appreciated, even enjoyed his many performances of original songs and improvised "operas" during the years of sessions. The special, invented languages in his "operas" reflected, I think, an awareness of the special nature of language in therapy that is different than that of language in external reality. In other words, it was a playfulness that sustained the essentially paradoxical framework of the analytic process, the paradox that things can be real and not real at the same time.

Play in the Analysis of a Rageful Adolescent Boy

Steve came to residential treatment after being abandoned by both of his parents. He had witnessed the mother's sexual promiscuity and drug abuse, as well as the suicide of an older sister. Subsequently abandoned by the father, who was schizophrenic and homeless, Steve later suffered sexual abuse from an uncle while in foster care with relatives. After an extended period of hopeless anger and rage in analytic treatment, Steve eventually began to regain a capacity to become increasingly playful with me, both with objects and with fantasy stories. His play began to reflect an ascendance of increasingly mutual and creative feelings, and some diminishment of his earlier preoccupations with themes of difference, rivalry, and revenge.

One of his first "invented games" involved a set of small plastic cowboys and Indians with their horses. At first, the game centered on arranging all of the horses with their rear ends pointed at me, and then they would all "fart" at me. This expression of anal aggressiveness toward me as an oedipal figure provided Steve with immense feelings of glee (given that his own father had been a ghost figure in his life, and too sick now to be the real target of such hostility). This was, I think, also reflective of a kind of paradox about which Pizer (1992, p. 233) has written. Steve's act was also associated with his need to grieve the loss of his father. I could not be his father. Yet, paradoxically, in a way that was also utterly true, Steve had to become like a son to whom, in my own countertransference, I could feel like a father. Subsequently, the game was transformed into an exhibition of Steve's fine-motor agility, when he built a precariously tall, free-standing tower with the horses and human figures–still a phallic configuration, but metaphorically expressive to me of his wish to achieve psychic balance.

Many sessions later, Steve came into the session, lay on the couch, and announced that he and I were "going out." "Where are we going?" I asked. "Oh, to a really fun place, you'll like it a lot!" Steve responded in mischievous tone. Then, with a sense of great excitement, Steve fantasized about how he and I would go out to a nightclub that he owned, "Steve's Rock and Roll Club." The club featured female dancers on stage–topless and bottomless (and, he assured me, that didn't mean that the tops and bottoms of their bodies were missing, but that they were nude dancers). Of course, Steve mused, there are many nude dance clubs in America, but his was very, very special. And because it was so special, he and I would have the best of times there. "How is Steve's Rock and Roll Club so different?" I asked. He responded that it was unique because everyone could "relate" to each other–the patrons could "relate" to the nude dancers on stage, but, more important, the patrons, especially he and I, could also "relate" to each other.

Our trip to Steve's Rock and Roll Club lasted for a number of sessions, and in those sessions Steve decided to build a number of additions to the club, so that we would never really have to leave it. The nightclub became an interconnected mall-like structure, providing for many of our needs, not just for relating and attachment. After the nightclub closed we would go to "Steve's

Restaurant" (for nourishment-nurturance), then to the health and fitness club, then drop our party clothes off at "Steve's Laundry and Dry Cleaners" (even if we partied together all night, we had to maintain a sense of respectability), and then we would finally retire for a good day's sleep at "Steve's Motel" before returning to the Rock and Roll Club the next night. This illustration of his communication through play involving the use of intersubjective, creative verbal fantasy reflected the sometimes quite noticeable erotic tone of his discourse, play, and transference feelings toward me. Further, it provided a convincing example of how the sexual, sensual, or eroticized transference may have many meanings (in this case, the repetition of the sexually charged atmosphere of early life experiences with his mother, wishes regarding me, feelings about the therapeutic relationship as potentially capable of transforming his earlier eroticized life experiences, the atmosphere of our sessions, and the residential milieu in general), in addition to the *manifest* sexual one (Klein, 1969; Lachmann, 1994).

Another example of his multifaceted communication through play involved some battery-operated motors, batteries, small light bulbs, and erector set parts that he brought to session some weeks later. He wanted to make the "fastest motors" and "brightest lights" that I'd ever seen. As he worked at constructing the various light and motor gadgets, he engaged in the following commentary toward me, which could hardly, among other things, be a less direct appeal for me to function as a soothing, admiring, mirroring self-object for him. "Watch me, watch me . . . you'll think I'm such a genius. Now I'm going to make this great light switch . . . Steve's switch . . . you're gonna love this; you're gonna love this. And now I'm going to make the awesomest 'thingamadigger' . . . 'thingamadicker' . . . a motorized propeller with a switch. And this is the wire connecting to the battery . . . connecting wire . . . and I'm gonna stick this wire right up your butt!" That eroticized part of his associations could be understood from a number of perspectives: once again as an expression of wishes for connection and attachment, of aggressive sexual feelings, and of the possible or potential fusion of both those wishes. Further, the "connecting wire" may well have been an allusion to the actual sexual abuse he suffered in childhood, which did in fact involve the application of electrical shocks to his genitals.

Much later, during a session near the very end of termination, Steve suddenly became very quiet and, while glancing toward me with an air of endearment, murmured, "Sweet. . . ." "Sweet?" I asked. "Yes," he replied, "like chocolate." Then Steve launched into a dramatic oration of certain parts of one of his favorite movies, *Forrest Gump*, recapturing the real actor's performance to a degree that was truly stunning to me. However, as I listened more closely to selections of his performance, I remembered that some of the major themes of *Forrest Gump* included the difficulties of the lives of the socially marginal and the issue of whether life is simply a matter of fate, or whether it also essentially involves the choices made. Perhaps even more fundamentally, the movie was concerned with how one human being, while coping with significant social or functional impairments, could manage a number of separations, losses, and endings in his important caretaking and love relationships. "Chocolate, sweet cho-co-late," Steve repeated to me. I remembered that the first reference to chocolate occurred at the beginning of the movie as Forrest sat with a box of chocolates and recalled that his mother had once told him, "Life is like a box of chocolates, you never know what you're gonna get." Of course, by the end of the movie, Forrest realized that while we may not know ahead of time what we will get, it is not all simply a matter of fate. For Steve also, there had been a realization that beyond the fact of his early traumatic experiences, he could begin to take the direction of his life into his own hands.

CONCLUSION

This paper began with a discussion of some of the early, historical writings about the use of play in child analysis, and continued with a theoretical discussion regarding certain aspects of play as a continuous and basic function in psychoanalysis. This included a consideration of some of the more general implications of play as non-linear versus non-play as linear, in terms of selected views about essentialist versus more relational, constructivist approaches to treatment. In line with the position that play is an essential process of both child and adult treatment, the paper then presented case material that described both the physical and verbal elements of play, which were important processes of communication and growth in the analytic treatment of two young persons in longer-term residential care at the Sonia Shankman Orthogenic School at the University of Chicago. The vignettes presented from both cases illustrated the use of play as non-linear, taking different forms, and constructivist in the play space that some have called the "Third," or the "sense" of the analytic experience.

REFERENCES

Abrams, S. (1999) How child and adult analysis inform and misinform one another. In: *Annual of Psychoanalysis*, 26-27 (J. A. Winer, Ed.), pp. 3-20. The Analytic Press: Hillsdale, NJ/London.

Altman, N. (1997) The case of Ronald: Oedipal issues in the treatment of a seven-year-old boy. *Psychoanalytic Dialogues, 7* (6), 725-739.

Bettelheim, B. (1950) *Love Is Not Enough*. Free Press: New York.

Bettelheim, B. (1955) *Truants from Life.* Free Press: New York.
Bettelheim, B. (1974) *A Home for the Heart.* Alfred A. Knopf: New York.
Frankel, J. B. (1998) The play's the thing: How the essential processes of therapy are seen most clearly in child therapy. *Psychoanalytic Dialogues, 8* (1), 149-182.
Freud, A. (1946/1964) *The Psychoanalytical Treatment of Children.* Schocken Books: New York.
Ghent, E. (1992) Paradox and process. *Psychoanalytic Dialogues, 2* (2), 135-159.
Gill, M. M. (1994) *Psychoanalysis in Transition.* The Analytic Press: Hillsdale, NJ/London.
Hoffman, I. Z. (1987) The value of uncertainty in psychoanalytic practice. *Contemporary Psychoanalysis, 23* (2), 205-215.
Hoffman, I. Z. (1998) *Ritual and Spontaneity in Psychoanalysis.* The Analytic Press: Hillsdale, NJ/London.
Klein, G. (1969) Freud's two theories of sexuality. In: *Psychology versus Metapsychology: Psychological Issues* (Gill, M. M. & Holzman, P., Eds.), pp. 14-70. International Universities Press: New York.
Klein, M. (1932) *The Psycho-Analysis of Children.* The Hogarth Press: London.
Lachmann, F. M. (1994) How can I eroticize thee? Let me count the ways. *Psychoanalytic Inquiry, 14* (4), 604-621.
Lear, J. (1998) *Open Minded.* Harvard University Press: Cambridge, MA/London, pp. 16-32.
Mitchell, S. A. (1991) Wishes, needs, and interpersonal negotiations. *Psychoanalytic Inquiry, 11,* 147-170.
Parsons, M. (1999) The logic of play in psychoanalysis. *International Journal of Psychoanalysis, 80* (5), 871-884.
Pizer, S. A. (1992) The negotiation of paradox in the analytic process. *Psychoanalytic Dialogues, 2* (2), 215-240.
Winnicott, D. W. (1971/1991) *Playing and Reality.* Routledge: London and New York.
Zimmerman, D. P. (1999) Scientism and managed care: The betrayal of group and individual treatment for children. *Therapeutic Communities, 20* (4), 281-300.
Zimmerman, D. P. (2000) Psychotherapy in residential treatment: The human toll of scientism and managed care. *Residential Treatment for Children and Youth, 18* (2), 55-85.
Zimmerman, D. P., & Cohler, B. J. (1998) From disciplinary control to benign milieu in children's residential treatment. *Therapeutic Communities, 19* (2), 123-146.

BIOGRAPHICAL NOTE

D. Patrick Zimmerman, PsyD, is Assistant Director, Admissions and Psychotherapy Services, The Sonia Shankman Orthogenic School. He is also Lecturer, The Department of Psychiatry and The Committee on Human Development, The University of Chicago. In addition, he serves as a member of the Senior Associate Core Faculty at the Illinois School of Professional Psychology/Chicago. He is a graduate of the Chicago Center for Psychoanalysis and a member of the CCP Board of Directors.

Reconsidering Classic Case Studies:
The "Mechanical Boy" and the "Space Child"

Richard A. Epstein, Jr., MA

SUMMARY. Bruno Bettelheim and Rudolph Ekstein are two of the early seminal figures in the field of residential treatment for severely emotionally disturbed children and adolescents. Many of their published works included detailed examinations of clinical case material and discussions that involved explorations of the therapeutic use of meaning and metaphor in the behaviors and communications of psychotic children. The current paper revisits their respective classic case studies, "Joey: A Mechanical Boy" and "Tommy the Space Child," as well as discusses the implications of contemporary relational theory for using the meaning and metaphor of behaviors and communications described in classic case studies and, by extension, to other clinical situations. *[Article copies available for a fee from The Haworth Document Delivery Service: 1-800-HAWORTH. E-mail address: <docdelivery@haworthpress.com> Website: <http://www.HaworthPress.com> © 2003 by The Haworth Press, Inc. All rights reserved.]*

KEYWORDS. Bettelheim, Ekstein, case studies, meaning and metaphor, and relational theory

The author may be written at: The Sonia Shankman Orthogenic School at the University of Chicago, 1365 East 60th Street, Chicago, IL 60637.

[Haworth co-indexing entry note]: "Reconsidering Classic Case Studies: The 'Mechanical Boy' and the 'Space Child.' " Epstein, Richard A., Jr. Co-published simultaneously in *Residential Treatment for Children & Youth* (The Haworth Press, Inc.) Vol. 20, No. 4, 2003, pp. 43-52; and: *Psychotherapy in Group Care: Making Life Good Enough* (ed: D. Patrick Zimmerman et al.) The Haworth Press, Inc., 2003, pp. 43-52. Single or multiple copies of this article are available for a fee from The Haworth Document Delivery Service [1-800-HAWORTH, 9:00 a.m. - 5:00 p.m. (EST). E-mail address: docdelivery@haworthpress.com].

43

INTRODUCTION

Some time ago I was participating in a clinical case conference for a schizo-phrenic adolescent girl in residential treatment. Her teacher told a story about how shortly after an incident in which the girl had desperately tried to return to her dormitory during the school day (which is not allowed), she began talking about an imaginary trip to Disney World that she hoped to take with her mother. In her desperation, the girl had urinated on herself and although that proved an effective strategy for being allowed to return to her dormitory to clean up and change clothes, it was, I imagine, a humiliating experience for her. Nevertheless, we quickly dismissed the girl's subsequent talk about a fantasy trip to the "magical kingdom" as further evidence of her deteriorated mental state and after the teacher remarked about what the girl had said, our group moved on to other topics.

Although I do not think that our dismissal of what the girl said is particularly unusual in the current landscape of residential treatment for severely emotionally disturbed children and adolescents, it does stand in marked contrast to the detailed examinations of meaning and metaphor in clinical case material that formed much of the basis of many of the early scholarly contributions on the residential treatment process. In the paper that follows, I will briefly review two of the classic clinical case studies, Bettelheim's "mechanical boy" and Ekstein's "space child," and reconsider those cases from a contemporary relational psychodynamic perspective.

REVIEWING "JOEY: A MECHANICAL BOY" AND "THE SPACE CHILD"

Bruno Bettelheim and Rudolph Ekstein are two of the early seminal figures in the field of residential treatment for severely emotionally disturbed children and adolescents. Working respectively at the Sonia Shankman Orthogenic School at the University of Chicago and at the Southard School of the Menninger Clinic in Topeka, Kansas, they were colleagues, friends and competitors. Between them, they wrote many books and published many articles about residential treatment with severely emotionally disturbed children and adolescents. Many of those books and articles include detailed examinations of clinical case material. Those discussions involved explorations of the therapeutic use of meaning and metaphor in the behaviors and communications of psychotic children.

Their classic case studies, "Joey: A Mechanical Boy" (Bettelheim, 1956, 1967) and "The Space Child" (Ekstein, 1952, 1966), presented quite detailed discussions of the therapeutic use of meaning and metaphor in working with severely disturbed children in residential care. Although both did so from the classical-Freudian, drive-centered psychoanalytic perspective characteristic of their era, the main difference between their approaches was that Bettelheim discussed clinical material based on observations of Joey in the residential milieu, while

Ekstein's discussions focused on Tommy's individual psychotherapeutic relationship while he was in residential treatment.

In the case of Joey, Bettelheim (1956) discussed how the wartime circumstances of the family into which Joey was born impacted the parents' readiness for parenthood. Neither parent was prepared or excited about Joey's arrival. The father, due to the war, was often not available. The mother viewed Joey as additional household work and burden. He was fed and toilet trained on a strict schedule. As Bettelheim explained, Joey's toilet training brought his mother neither feelings of success nor accomplishment. It simply saved her time in the same manner as properly functioning household appliances.

Given this summary of Bettelheim's view of Joey's early upbringing, it will perhaps not be surprising that Bettelheim's case presentation focused on Joey's delusional fantasy about the role of machines in running his body and, specifically, upon the child's difficulties regarding the process of elimination. The boy's machinery was quite elaborate. Made from cardboard, masking tape, and other "odds and ends," his manufactured carburetors and engines kept him running. He had an elaborate system of "plugging himself in" to an imaginary outlet with an imaginary wire and then "insulating" himself with napkins so that his digestive apparatuses could properly function.

There was another aspect of Joey's behavior, however, that was equally confusing. Joey would function for days on end without incident and then suddenly explode, destroying his machinery and anything else within his reach. Bettelheim explained that the milieu gradually came to understand that Joey "had created these machines to run his body and mind because it was too painful to be human. But again and again he became dissatisfied with their failure to meet his need and rebellious at the way they frustrated his will" (p. 122). They were, according to Bettelheim, Joey's attempts not only to deal with having a mother who did not want to be bothered with him, but also to protect himself against inevitable feelings of aggression and social isolation.

Bettelheim also described in considerable detail the complicated procedures that were involved in Joey's toileting routines. As Bettelheim described, "We had to accompany him; he had to take off all his clothes; he could only squat, not sit, on the toilet seat; he had to touch the wall with one hand, in which he also clutched frantically the vacuum tubes that powered his elimination. He was terrified lest his whole body be sucked down" (p. 122). To aid in making his elimination routine less elaborate, the milieu began providing Joey with a metal wastebasket to use in lieu of a toilet, and over time he became able not to need to take off all of his clothes, to hold onto a wall, or to be accompanied by an adult.

Bettelheim (1956) stated, "It was not simply that his parents had subjected him to rigid, early training. Many children are so trained. But in most cases the parents have a deep emotional investment in the child's performance. The child's response in turn makes training an occasion for interaction between them and for the building of genuine relationships. . . . So it had been with all other aspects of Joey's existence with his parents" (p. 124).

In the case of Tommy, the "space child," Ekstein (1952) discussed how the parents held positions of prominence in a North American city. They were described, in contrast to Joey's parents, not as rejecting of Tommy, but as emotionally distant and unavailable. In addition, Tommy had experienced severe asthma from a very young age, and at the time of his admission to the Southard School of the Menninger Clinic the asthma was the parents' primary concern.

Again, given the picture of the parents and Tommy's early upbringing, it was not surprising to Ekstein that the child developed delusional fantasies about and expressed his understanding of his own difficulties in terms of metaphors of distance. Initially, he discussed fantasies in which "he was a Five-Star General, commanded countless space ships, was out to destroy the world, sailed to faraway regions of space, destroyed stars and invaded different solar systems" (p. 212). These fantastic images were in stark contrast to the reality of the child's presentation as a scared and frightened little boy. In the individual therapy, Tommy spoke of the battles– both victories and defeats- that occurred light years away, deep into outer space.

As Ekstein (1952) wrote, "The psychotherapist's main concern was with the distance between the psychological world of this faraway monster and that of the little fellow who was yearning to be loved and accepted by his parents, by the children and the teachers in the school" (p. 214). After some time, the therapist suggested to Tommy that perhaps the old general could come down to earth once he felt that it was clear that no one could defeat him. Some time shortly thereafter, Tommy arrived in session announcing that he was no longer Tommy, but was now a boy named "Oscar Pumphandle," who was a friend of Tommy's. Tommy, it turned out, had moved to the Arizona desert to make and test atomic bombs.

The point that Ekstein wanted his readers to notice is that although the split between the timid, fearful boy and the aggressive, powerful monster was still a great distance, it had become a much, much smaller one and also that it was Tommy who had become dangerous, as opposed to his "alter-ego." It was not until Tommy indicated that he had an awareness that the metaphor of distance was being used as a defense (by recognizing the silly name he gave to Oscar as a joke and joking as a way to distance) that the therapist suggested to him that per- haps Tommy and Oscar weren't friends after all and that perhaps Oscar was afraid of what would happen if Tommy came back.

Tommy came back and was an absolute terror. As Ekstein wrote about the child's behavior in therapy and in the residential milieu more generally, "Tommy was at first as helplessly exposed to his own inner impulses as the therapist was to his aggressive, provoking behavior. . . . The child attempted to openly masturbate during psychotherapeutic hours, began to steal and to destroy equipment, blew up car tires, expressed hate for staff members, organized gangs with the other children, and turn from a timid youngster into a vicious little monster" (p. 215). The problem of the treatment had become a problem of how to show Tommy that the milieu was strong enough to protect him from his own destructiveness and thereby prove to him that he did not need to retreat to his defensive position, now in Arizona.

After several weeks of his destructiveness and of the milieu's attempts to contain it, Tommy began to talk with the therapist about himself and his parents. Although from time to time he slipped into his "distance fantasies," they were now fantasies of time involving dinosaurs instead of fantasies of space. He also began to be able to talk directly with his therapist about sex and sexual temptations.

CLASSICAL UNDERSTANDINGS OF THE "MECHANICAL BOY" AND "SPACE CHILD"

Although not explicitly stated, the authors' clear implications were that the children's experiences of pathogenic care early in life probably had etiological force in determining the their difficulties. The presumption was that a lack of emotional involvement on the part of the parents led both to an impaired ability for the child to relate to others, as well as to the use of certain defensive strategies (e.g., metaphoric communications or delusional fantasies about mechanization, in Joey's case, and about distance in time and space, in Tommy's case) to protect oneself against and to help make sense of the experienced isolation.

The authors presumed that the readers shared their assumption that a lack of parental emotional involvement led to impaired relations and, at times, defensive compensatory grandiose fantasies of strength. The presumption seemed to be that this lack of parental emotional involvement was directly related to the child's later inability or ineffective attempts to manage primitive sexual and aggressive impulses, an assumption that would most likely have been shared by many of their readers at the time.

In the case of Joey, the lack of emotional involvement on the part of the parents in an important aspect of the child's life led to a situation where the child attempted to satisfy and protect himself from his primitive sexual and aggressive impulses through elaborate procedures designed to make his own existence more machine-like. In the case of Tommy, the lack of emotional availability on the part of the parents, combined with the child's poor physical condition, led to a situation where the child distanced himself from his primitive sexual and aggressive impulses through the process of splitting and elaborate defensive fantasies about faraway places and times.

In the classic presentations of case material contained within the stories of Joey and Tommy we see both the marked similarities and contrasting approaches of each of the authors. Bettelheim (1956, 1967) based his case study on the anecdotal notes of staff in the residential milieu and upon his own observations, while Ekstein (1952, 1966) based his case study on the notes of the child's individual psychotherapist. These contrasting approaches, which may be more reflective of differences in emphasis or perspective, illustrate the wealth of clinical material that residential treatment with emotionally disturbed children has to offer. They also illustrate that there are at least several ways of framing that clinical material in a manner that can be understood by others. Another important aspect of the manner in which the authors framed the case material, one which they share not only with each other but also with other authors from their era, is the classically-Freudian, one-person psychological language and conceptual focus.

Bettelheim's presentation of Joey the mechanical boy is characteristic of the classical-psychoanalytic, drive-centered interpretation of the clinical material typical of the era in which he wrote, focusing on primitive sexual and aggressive impulses and/or the defensive attempts to deal with them. Specific emphasis is placed upon Joey's destructive and toileting behaviors. Regarding his destructive behaviors, although Bettelheim and his staff came to understand them as expressing Joey's sense of frustration with the inadequacy of the machines running his life, it also seems to be that the machines were a defense against the overwhelming sense of anger that he felt towards his parents for their failings. Regarding his toileting behaviors, although Bettelheim states that Joey's personality is not "anal" in the Freudian sense, he also spent a remarkable amount of time discussing the boy's obsession with the process of elimination and what his fixation on this process might mean.

Ekstein's presentation of Tommy the space child is an equally classical-psychoanalytic, drive-centered interpretation and equally characteristic of the thinking of the era. Ekstein focused on the process of splitting, as it was used by Tommy to separate his primitively aggressive characteristics from himself as a meek and timid child in reality. He focused on the boy's use of the metaphor of distance as a way of defending himself and those around him from that primitive aggression. Later in the course of the individual therapy, after Tommy had made progress in shortening the distance between the two aspects of his personality, Ekstein turned his attention to Tommy's attempts to manage his primitive sexual impulses. It was in mastering these within the context of his transference to his female therapist that Tommy was eventually able to begin discussing his relationship with his parents in a meaningful manner.

CONTEMPORARY RELATIONAL RECONSIDERATIONS

Both Bettelheim and Ekstein wrote about their cases from the classical-Freudian, one-person, drive-centered perspective of their era. In accordance with that perspective, they focused their case studies upon discussions of primitive sexual and aggressive impulses and defenses against them.

Among the differences between drive-centered and relational approaches are that relational approaches pay more attention to the transference/countertransference interaction, view the analyst/therapist as a potentially "new" object for the child based on their interactions in the here-and-now, and emphasize the patient's situatedness within social, cultural, and historical contexts (Altman, Briggs, Frankel, Gensler, & Pantone, 2002; Fairbairn, 1952, 1958; Hoffman, 1998; Mitchell, 1988). Three-person psychologies–the three "people" being the patient, the analyst, and the context within which the therapeutic relationship occurs–developed from the growing recognition in analytic work with patients of the inherent impossibility of analyst, neutrality and the inherent situatedness of individuals within context (Altman, 1995; Fairbairn, 1952, 1958).

Perhaps the most obvious change in theoretical perspective is the change from transference as distortion of reality-based relationship with the analyst to include the possibility of transference as based, at least in part, on the patient's real experience of the analyst (Hoffman, 1998). As Hoffman (1998) states, "Those of us . . . who have been trying to work out a 'constructivist' view of the analytic process . . . are faced with the necessity of coming to grips with the full implications of that perspective for the role of the analyst in the patient's life. If we believe that the analyst is involved in the construction rather than *merely* the discovery of the patient's psychic reality, we are confronted with the fact that, according to that view, there is no affective attunement that is merely responsive to and reflective of what the patient brings to the situation" (p. 75). In other words, the analyst is an inherent part of the patient's relational matrix or social world and cannot be more simply be regarded as being above or, at least, outside of it.

In the cases of Joey and Tommy, Bettelheim and Ekstein, respectively, approached the relationship between analyst and child in the traditional manner characteristic of their era. Issues of transference took a back seat to issues of drive and when transference was considered, it was in the sense of the patient projecting onto the analyst whatever conflictual thoughts and feelings were at the center of their difficulties. The analysts' role in the transference process was that of a neutral receptacle for distorted projections. In Joey's case, Bettelheim wrote about his machinery and other "preventions" without conveying a sense of how the interactions between milieu staff and child work to mutually constitute Joey's reality. For Tommy, Ekstein equally conveyed the sense that the analyst/therapist was simply a neutral interpreter of Tommy's experience, not a person engaged in a mutually constructed relationship with Tommy.

The analyst's potential as a "new" object is also more heavily emphasized in contemporary relational perspectives than it was by Bettelheim or Ekstein in their case discussions. Although both hinted at the potential for the residential milieu or individual therapist to respond to the child in a manner that provides him/her with new interpersonal experiences, contemporary relational theory pays explicit attention to this potential. The reasons why explicit attention is paid may perhaps best be explained by considering Fairbairn's reinterpretation of Freudian theory.

Fairbairn (1952, 1958) argued that libido, the force behind Freudian drive theory, is less pleasure seeking, as Freud had argued, than it is object seeking. In his view, the primary motivating force in human life is not the attainment of pleasure, but the establishment and maintenance of relationships with other people. Further, people establish relational patterns early in life and repeat those patterns in future relationships not only because they are familiar with those patterns, but also because doing so serves the purpose of keeping those early relationships "alive" at least as a psychological reality. In terms of the theoretical psychotherapeutic relationship (and, by extension, relationships within the therapeutic residential milieu), the analyst, then, has the potential to intuit relational patterns and to decide the extent to which to allow those patterns to continue in the context of transference/countertransference interactions. The extent to which the analyst is able not to allow those patterns to continue in the psychotherapeutic relationship is directly related to the extent to which the analyst may represent a "new" object, or relational other, to the patient.

Finally, although Bettelheim and Ekstein suggested an awareness of the child's embeddedness within social, cultural, and historical contexts, they did not emphasize the interactive quality of this situatedness. Bettelheim and Ekstein hinted at such a conception when they discussed the deleterious impact of the relational field in which Joey and Tommy, respectively, spent their early days. In doing so, however, they placed their emphasis on the etiological force of poor parenting rather than on the interactive nature of the relationship between these children and their environments.

Contemporary relational theorists stress the interactive and mutually constructive nature of an individual's inherent location within social, cultural, and historical context. As Mitchell (1988) states, "For relational-model theorists, as for the modern anthropologist and the modern linguist, the individual mind is a *product* of as well as an interactive participant in the cultural, linguistic matrix within which it comes into being. Meaning is not provided a priori, but derives from the relational matrix. The relational field is constitutive of individual experience" (p. 19). Bettelheim and Ekstein demonstrated an understanding of the embedded nature of human existence in some of their other writings describing the residential milieu in painstaking detail (e.g., Bettelheim, 1950). It is only through a thorough understanding of the proximal context of the children's lives in the milieu that the authors were able to make sense of the meaning and metaphor present within the children's behaviors and other communications.

In summary, contemporary relational psychodynamic theories suggest that people are inherently situated within a field of relationships and interpersonal interactions and that the inherent nature of this embedded state makes it difficult and misleading to talk about human development and its vicissitudes without recognizing the mutually constructive relationship between individuals' internal and social worlds. The implications of this type of theoretical view of human existence for the psychotherapeutic enterprise, whether focusing on relationships within a therapeutic residential milieu or on an individual psychotherapeutic relationship, involve enhanced attention to the analyst/therapist's role in the patient's social world and to the context of the patient's life. As I hope my application of contemporary relational perspectives to the cases presented by Bettelheim and Ekstein have shown, their attention to precisely the same details that contemporary relational theory emphasizes allows for consideration of the meaning and metaphor in clinical material.

DISCUSSION

The current paper reviewed two of the classic discussions of clinical case material from the residential treatment of schizophrenic children and presented a brief reconsideration of those cases from a contemporary relational psychodynamic perspective. The shift from concerns about primitive sexual and aggressive impulses and the attempts to negotiate and defend against those impulses has resulted in a dramatic revision of classically Freudian, one-person psychologies.

In the cases of Joey and Tommy, unlike that of the schizophrenic adolescent I mentioned in the introduction, paying attention to meaning and metaphor in the behavior and communications of psychotic children can lead to a better understanding of their internal worlds and provide insight into possible interventions. Indeed, in the brief description of the girl's behavior in my introduction, her trip to the dormitory during the school day, and the efforts she had made to get there, are elaborate in a manner similar to the types of preparations one makes for a vacation. It may be that she felt communicating through metaphor to be a safer way to try to begin to talk about an experience subjectively apprehended as humiliating. It may also be that an attempt to communicate with her on the level of metaphor would be a beneficial way for her to begin to explore her otherwise overtly psychotic behaviors. It seems to me a sad commentary on the current state of residential treatment for many severely emotionally disturbed children and adolescents that few professionals continue to involve themselves in the inner fantasy worlds of the children with whom they work.

As I hope my reconsideration of two of the classic case studies of residential treatment with severely emotionally disturbed children shows, the importance of meaning and metaphor in the behavior and communications of psychotic children can continue to play an important role, even in cases conceptualized from more contemporary theoretical perspectives.

REFERENCES

Altman, N. (1995). *The Analyst in the Inner City: Race, Class, and Culture Through a Psychoanalytic Lens*. Hillsdale, NJ: The Analytic Press.

Altman, N., Briggs, R., Frankel, J., Gensler, D., & Pantone, P. (2002). *Relational Child Psychotherapy*. New York: Other Press.

Bettelheim, B. (1950). *Love Is Not Enough*. Glencoe, IL: The Free Press.

Bettelheim, B. (1959). Joey: A mechanical boy. *Scientific American*, 200(3), 116-127.

Bettelheim, B. (1967). *The Empty Fortress: Infantile Autism and the Birth of the Self*. New York: The Free Press.

Ekstein, R. (1966). *Children of Time and Space: Clinical Studies on the Psychoanalytic Treatment of Severely Disturbed Children*. New York: Appleton-Century-Crofts.

Ekstein, R., & Wright, D. (1952). The space child. *Bulletin of the Menninger Clinic*, 16, 211-224.

Fairbairn, W.R.D. (1952). *An Object-Relations Theory of the Personality*. New York: Basic Books.

Fairbairn, W.R.D. (1958). On the nature and aims of psycho-analytical treatment. *International Journal of Psychoanalysis*, 39, 374-385.

Hoffman, I.Z. (1998). *Ritual and Spontaneity in the Psychoanalytic Process: A Dialectical-Constructivist View*. Hillsdale, NJ: The Analytic Press.

Mitchell, S. (1988). *Relational Concepts in Psychoanalysis: An Integration*. Cambridge: Harvard University Press.

BIOGRAPHICAL NOTE

Richard A. Epstein, Jr., MA, received his master's degree from and is currently a doctoral candidate in the Committee on Human Development in the Department of Psychology at the University of Chicago. He is a Program Manager at the Sonia Shankman Orthogenic School at the University of Chicago and Managing Editor of *Residential Treatment for Children & Youth*.

Alice's Loss of Wonderland

Richard A. Epstein, Jr., MA

SUMMARY. The current paper discusses issues of transference and countertransference in a psychodynamic psychotherapy of an emotionally disturbed girl in residential treatment. The paper argues that unrecognized rescue fantasies may underlie the strong negative feelings evoked in the countertransference and that projective identification may then be used as a defense against those feelings. The paper also argues that the current emphasis on providing short-term, empirically validated, and cost-effective treatments for emotionally disturbed children and adolescents may be producing residential child-care workers and institutions that are even less prepared to recognize and work through the difficult feelings evoked in the process of working with emotionally disturbed and disturbing young people. *[Article copies available for a fee from The Haworth Document Delivery Service: 1-800-HAWORTH. E-mail address: <docdelivery@haworthpress.com> Website: <http://www.HaworthPress.com> © 2003 by The Haworth Press, Inc. All rights reserved.]*

KEYWORDS. Transference, countertransference, rescue fantasies, projective identification, child psychotherapy, child-care workers

As anyone who works in a residential treatment center knows, there has been great pressure for some time from third party funding sources to limit the

The author may be written at: The Sonia Shankman Orthogenic School at the University of Chicago, 1365 East 60th Street, Chicago, IL 60637.

[Haworth co-indexing entry note]: "Alice's Loss of Wonderland." Epstein, Richard A., Jr. Co-published simultaneously in *Residential Treatment for Children & Youth* (The Haworth Press, Inc.) Vol. 20, No. 4, 2003, pp. 53-72; and: *Psychotherapy in Group Care: Making Life Good Enough* (ed: D. Patrick Zimmerman et al.) The Haworth Press, Inc., 2003, pp. 53-72. Single or multiple copies of this article are available for a fee from The Haworth Document Delivery Service [1-800-HAWORTH, 9:00 a.m. - 5:00 p.m. (EST). E-mail address: docdelivery@haworthpress.com].

http://www.haworthpress.com/store/product.asp?sku=J007
© 2003 by The Haworth Press, Inc. All rights reserved.
10.1300/J007v20n04_04

use of residential treatment settings for emotionally disturbed children and adolescents (e.g., Eisikovitis & Schwartz, 1991). An optimistic perspective is that the pressure may represent a strong belief in the ability to treat emotionally disturbed children and adolescents on an outpatient basis within the school, family, and community. A less favorable perspective is that the pressure may reflect the predominance of managed care concerns for fiscal responsibility and the accompanying preference for short-term, empirically validated treatments.

The short-term, empirically validated treatments that are preferred tend to be cognitive, behavioral, cognitive-behavioral, and psycho-educational in nature. Several authors have suggested that a pervasive, underlying scientism with objectivist assumptions about what count as "facts" has colluded with the monetarily driven concern for short-term treatments to counter more psychodynamic forms of treatment (e.g., Zimmerman, 2000a). In the case of residential treatment for emotionally disturbed children and adolescents, that collusion may be particularly problematic because it may work to produce residential institutions and child-care workers particularly ill-equipped to deal with phenomena that are not easily objectifiable, such as issues of transference and countertransference in the treatment process.

In psychodynamic schools of thought, it has long been acknowledged that transference and countertransference reactions can influence a therapist's decisions (Zimmerman & Cohler, 1998) and that unbridled countertransference reactions can significantly impact a patient's symptoms for the worse (Stanton & Schwartz, 1954). Zimmerman (1999) has described how the call for a more limited use of residential treatment may in and of itself reflect the presence of unusually intense transference and countertransference reactions towards residential institutions.

The current paper is a discussion of the psychodynamically oriented individual psychotherapy with an extremely troubled young girl in residential treatment. It is a highly selective presentation of case material that has been selected in order to discuss how social context interacts with individual dynamics and how these interactions are expressed through the child's transference and countertransference reactions. This is the case of a child, who despite encouraging response in individual psychotherapy, continued to display behaviors that were unmanageable in the residential and classroom settings and who must be considered a failed case of individual treatment in the residential facility.

Although the presentation of the clinical material in this case study suggests a relational and transference-oriented treatment approach, the purpose of the present study is to demonstrate the myriad of ways in which this child's residential treatment may have been negatively impacted by the inability of the residential staff, classroom staff, and individual therapist to effectively deal with issues related to transference and countertransference.

BACKGROUND INFORMATION

Alice entered residential treatment at the Sonia Shankman Orthogenic School at the University of Chicago when she was eight years old.[1] For many years, the Orthogenic School's treatment philosophy was based on psychoanalytic ideas about milieu therapy (e.g., Bettelheim, 1950, 1955, 1967, 1974; Bettelheim & Sylvester, 1947, 1948; Sanders, 1989; Zimmerman, 1990, 1994, 2000b); more recently the school has incorporated cognitive, behavioral, cognitive-behavioral, psycho-educational, and pharmacological perspectives into its treatment philosophy. Alice was in treatment at the school for approximately three years. During that time she lived in one of the school's all-girl dormitories, attended classes in one of the school's self-contained, cross-categorical special education classrooms, met with the school's psychiatrist for psychotropic medication management once per month, and met with me for forty-five minute individual psychotherapy sessions twice each week.[2]

Alice's early life was filled with themes of caregiver rejection and abandonment. She was the oldest of three children born to a single mother who did not complete her high school education. When she was one and one-half years old, Alice and her siblings were removed from the home of their biological mother by a state child protection agency because of severe neglect and suspected physical and sexual abuse. The biological mother's parental rights were terminated shortly thereafter. Alice's biological father was a non-custodial parent at that time.

The state child protection agency initially placed Alice and her siblings with a female relative of their biological mother. After roughly three years (when Alice was approximately four years old), that placement failed because the relative's husband became abusive. Although the children were subsequently placed with a stable foster family, Alice began to display significant emotional and behavioral problems. She began to display sexual behaviors toward her biological and foster siblings, to lie, to steal, and, when she began attending school, to be suspended with regularity for misbehaving.

Alice's foster family sought individual psychotherapy and a formal sexual abuse evaluation for Alice when she was approximately six years old. It is likely that Alice had begun to display signs of an emotional or behavioral disturbance some period of time prior to the foster family seeking psychological services. Although it is not clear how consistent her contact was with the services she received at that time, it is clear that her emotional and behavioral difficulties persisted. When Alice was approximately seven and one-half years old the foster family notified the state child protection agency of their decision to adopt Alice's siblings, but not to adopt Alice. Alice was placed in another foster home and, when that placement also failed, in a children's shelter until arrangements could be made for Alice to enter residential treatment. At the time Alice entered residential treatment at the school, her problematic behaviors also included physically threatening and aggressive behaviors directed towards herself, her peers, and adult authority figures.

Psychological evaluations indicate that Alice tested in the Average range of intelligence. Examiners noted that Alice's emotional and attentional difficulties suggested that the intelligence testing results may have been underestimates of her true intellectual potential; that the emotional and attentional factors may have adversely effected her performance on the test tasks. Projective testing indicated impaired reality testing without the presence of a formal thought disorder, low self-esteem, and feelings of sadness, anxiety, and abandonment. Measures of adaptive behavior indicated that Alice's social and life skills lagged far behind those of her same age peers.

As is often the case with children who are profoundly disturbed, Alice had received numerous DSM-IV psychiatric diagnoses. These diagnoses included a Post-Traumatic Stress Disorder, a Reactive Attachment Disorder, a Major Depressive Disorder, an Attention Deficit-Hyperactivity Disorder (Hyperactive-Impulsive subtype), an Oppositional-Defiant Disorder, a Conduct Disorder, and persistent nocturnal enuresis.

PRE-RESIDENTIAL TREATMENT

Alice entered residential treatment at the school with a traumatic past and with severe emotional and behavioral difficulties that emerged at an early age. Her history was remarkable for the presence of severe neglect, suspected physical and sexual abuse at the hands of her family of origin and for the disruption of all subsequent primary caregiver relationships. Alice's history was also remarkable for the profundity and severity of her emotional and behavioral problems.

There is a significant literature about children who have experienced pathogenic care early in life and the disruptions of primary caregiver relationships that often accompany such care. From the perspective of psychiatric terminology, only some of those children will meet the formal criteria for either a Post-Traumatic Stress Disorder (PTSD) or a Reactive Attachment Disorder of Infancy or Early Childhood (RAD). Children who meet formal criteria for PTSD display "characteristic symptoms following exposure to an extreme traumatic stressor involving direct personal experience of an event that involves actual or threatened death or serious injury, or other threat to one's physical integrity . . . " (DSM-IV, American Psychiatric Association, 1994, pp. 424-429). Traumatic events are defined as, for example, military combat, violent personal assault, being kidnapped, or being taken hostage. Children who meet formal criteria for a RAD display "markedly disturbed and developmentally inappropriate social relatedness in most contexts, beginning before age 5 years"; these disturbances must not be accounted for exclusively by developmental delays and must be regarded as being the result of pathogenic care (DSM-IV, American Psychiatric Association, 1994, pp. 116-118).

The DSM-IV defines pathogenic care as "persistent disregard of the child's basic emotional needs for comfort, stimulation, and affection; persistent disregard of the child's basic physical needs; or repeated changes of primary caregiver that prevent formation of stable attachments (e.g., frequent changes in foster care)" (American Psychiatric Association, 1994, p. 116). Statistics on violence and children suggest that such pathogenic care is quite prevalent in the United States. For example, homicide is the third leading cause of death for children between the ages of 5 and 14 years (Ofosky, 1995), and there was a 300% increase in the number of children seriously injured by maltreatment between 1986 and 1993 (Children's Defense Fund, 1997). Unfortunately, infliction of such injuries is most often at the hands of a parent or primary caregiver.

Children who are victims of severely pathogenic care may be severely affected, and there has been a considerable amount of theorizing from many perspectives about the psychological consequences of such pathogenic care. One such line of theorizing attempts to delineate the consequences of disrupted attachment. As defined by Bowlby (1969) and Ainsworth (1973), attachment is "an enduring affective bond characterized by a tendency to seek and maintain proximity to a specific person, particularly when under stress" (Levy, 2000).

Although this definition is a primarily behavioral one, the psychological consequences of attachment are easily understood when its basic function for a young person is considered to be the provision of safety and a sense of security that accompanies being close, both physically and emotionally, to a caregiver. The positive consequences of appropriate attachment relationships may include: a more general sense of basic trust in other people and the world; an ability to explore the environment with a sense of safety and security; an ability to self-regulate impulses and emotions; an ability to form a sense of identity, self-worth, and autonomy; an ability to establish a moral framework; an ability to generate a positive core belief system about self, others, and the world more generally; and an ability to defend against stress and trauma (Levy & Orlans, 1995, 1998). However, if the caregiver does not adequately meet that need, then the child may develop a basic mistrust of other people and the world. The child who has experienced traumatizing relations with a primary caregiver, however, may not only have a basic mistrust of other people and, by extension, the world, but his or her expectations may also include aggressive, caustic, and hurtful ideas.

It should not, then, be surprising that a child like Alice, who has experienced trauma in and disruption of her attachments to her primary caregivers would display feelings of sadness and anxiety, as well as behaviors that were disorganized and aggressive. For that child, other people, and perhaps the whole world, are expected to act in a mean and hurtful manner. What looks like depression for that child may, moreover, represent the child's lack of confidence in the world. What looks like oppositional, defiant, and conduct-disordered behavior may more accurately portray a child who is full of rage and who is not a-moral, but, if you will permit the expression, pre-moral (Levy, 2000).

These observations may not only help explain the multiple DSM-IV psychiatric diagnoses that children like Alice receive, but may also help understand the types of thoughts and feelings that she may have been transferring onto the residential milieu and the adults who were in charge of her care while she was there. It may also help in beginning to try to understand the thoughts and feelings towards Alice of the School as an institution and of the particular adults who were in charge of her while she was there.

As shall become clear in the presentation that follows, Alice evoked strong reactions in the staff of the residential milieu. Indeed, she was a young girl in need of extraordinary amounts of care. For most of her stay at the School, for example, she was unable or unmotivated to participate in her own physical care (e.g., bathing, brushing teeth, combing hair) and reluctant to allow anyone to help her. Such a child uses up an enormous amount of staff resources and may generate in the staff feelings of being overwhelmed and engulfed by the child's needs. Combined with the child's lack of confidence in the world, primitive rage, and caustic expectations of her caregivers, the situation in the general milieu was ripe for severe countertransference reactions.

Ekstein, Wallerstein, and Mendelbaum (1992) point out in their discussion of countertransference reactions in the residential milieu that even staff who are supervised towards recognition of their own countertransference feelings often act out within the countertransference. They note that the milieu is particularly likely to evoke such reactions because the children have profound needs in multiple life domains, such as self-care skills, affect regulation, social relations, academic difficulties, etc., and the presence of multiple staff engagements. In their opinion, treatment fails when the child successfully brings about the same responses in the staff as he or she did in the family of origin or in earlier life.

INDIVIDUAL PSYCHOTHERAPY WITH ALICE

Alice began attending twice-weekly individual psychotherapy sessions approximately one month after her arrival to the school. Children are routinely allowed some period of time to adjust to the treatment milieu, to form relationships with the other children and members of the adult staff, prior to engaging in a one-on-one relationship with their therapist. During this initial phase of the residential treatment, Alice would often present herself to adults in an overly cute and engaging manner. Perhaps, as Cohen (1988) suggests, her "golden fantasy" was evoked. Subsequent to those first several weeks, however, it became increasingly clear that Alice was a very troubled child and she would frequently become extremely disorganized within the highly structured environment of the school.

At the beginning of individual psychotherapy, Alice seemed very excited about the possibility of having a one-to-one relationship with an adult in the school. For example, she would make a big show of my arrival to her classroom at her session time by loudly announcing my arrival, by making a scene of greeting me at the door and leaving the classroom with me. That experience was at the same time embarrassing because it disrupted whatever was happening in the classroom and flattering because it stoked my own narcissistic fires. Also, from the beginning, Alice seemed to have difficulties accepting that I was also the therapist for another young girl in her classroom and dormitory. Alice would often act aggressively towards this other child for no reason that was apparent to the adult staff. Although Alice could verbally express to me that she did not like this other girl because I was her therapist too, she did not seem to be able or willing to explore these ideas further or to change her behavior. After an incident in which Alice returned from her therapy session, she crossed the classroom and began choking the other girl. The school's crisis counselor mandated that Alice's transitions from her sessions with me back into her classroom include several minutes of sitting quietly outside the crisis counselor's office.

In session, Alice's demeanor was usually quite pleasant, although she consistently tested my limits. Initially, she would choose to spend her time with me drawing, resting on the couch, playing cards, and talking about concerns in her daily life. Alice required constant reminders to follow basic session rules (e.g., no touching, keeping the lights on). She was often also extremely disorganized during sessions (e.g., she would frequently try to jump from one activity to another). In addition, during our first several sessions together Alice would begin to make erotic motions while lying on the couch. Each time she engaged in such behavior, I calmly said, "Alice, you don't have to do that in here." Being aware of her history of abuse, I was hoping to communicate that I did not expect Alice to participate in activities like that when with me. After two or three sessions, she ceased such behavior.

After several months, therapy with Alice seemed to enter what might be called a second phase. Although Alice continued to have difficulties with the previously mentioned aspects of therapy, she seemed to become more comfortable with the therapy session routine and to accept the limits placed on her behavior by the basic session rules. For example, during this period of months Alice neither missed any sessions because she was out of the classroom with the crisis counselor, nor did she "misbehave" in sessions. During this phase of therapy Alice chose to spend the majority of her time in session engaging me in activities that were imaginative in nature (e.g., throwing tea parties for stuffed animals and playing with a doll house).

The recent literature supports including an element of play in therapy for traumatized children (e.g., Gaensbauer, 2000; Gil, 1991; Marvasti, 1993; Schaefer, 1994; Shelby, 2000) and play has always been an integral part of psychodynamic work with children. It has traditionally been regarded as the child treatment equivalent of dreams and free associations in work with adults (Altman, Briggs, Frankel, Gensler, & Pantone, 2002). From such a perspective, the child gives the therapist a glimpse of his/her inner world through play and the therapist offers interpretations.

Although Alice was playing during her sessions with me, I regarded play more broadly and was guided by more contemporary relational psychodynamic thought. My approach to Alice's play was that the act of playing could in and of itself be therapeutic. Altman et al. (2002) state that the result of play is "an interpersonal negotiation between the two participants regarding how the sessions are going to go, including the nature of the activities that the therapist and child will pursue" (p. 197). For Alice, play was a safe way for her to begin, albeit tentatively, to establish a new way of relating to an adult authority figure. It was also a way for me to begin to try to establish a trusting relationship with her that was based not upon my belief that I was a trustworthy person, but on our mutual interactions with one another in the here and now.

After approximately eight months at the school, Alice's behavior in the milieu began to seriously deteriorate. For example, the crisis counselors were called more than 50 times in one month, more than once per day, to help Alice's teacher and dormitory counselors manage her disruptive behaviors. Many, if not most of these calls, required the use of physical containment. As such, Alice missed several of her individual therapy sessions because she was with the crisis counselor during her session time. When she was able to attend session, Alice again began to test my limits by pressing the therapy session rules.

The deterioration of Alice's behavior in the milieu appeared to coincide with several events. For one, Alice's paternal grandfather began showing an interest in the possibility of becoming more actively involved in Alice's life. He began negotiating with the child welfare agency and began scheduling supervised visits to see Alice at the School. However, he would often fail to attend his scheduled visits with Alice. It may be that his sudden involvement in her life evoked difficult feelings for Alice. In line with Cohen's (1988) observations about the "golden fantasy," it may be that the reinvolvement of her family caused Alice to redirect her idealized fantasies back onto her family and her anger and hostility towards the residential institution. For another, several of Alice's dormitory counselors decided to leave the School. Their departure may have represented a repetition of past abandonment and inevitably disrupted the dormitory routine. Further, during the same period of months, remodeling of the School required me to conduct my therapy sessions in a new room in a different part of the School, thereby disrupting our session routine.

After the one-year anniversary of Alice's arrival at the School our work together entered what may be viewed as a third phase, which seemed, initially, to be marked by Alice having difficulties at the end of her therapy sessions. For example, Alice would often refuse to return to her classroom following our sessions, often throwing session room toys, throwing pillows, swearing, and hitting at me in ways that necessitated her missing her subsequent therapy session as a result. At one point, because of an incident in which Alice became quite aggressive towards me at the end of session, I began conducting Alice's sessions in a room closer to her classroom than my usual session room. This move was only temporary, as Alice quickly earned back my trust. I gradually came to understand these behaviors as communicating two things: first, that the relationship she had established with me was "better" than those she had in the classroom (hence the reluctance to return) and second, that the behaviors were also a way of testing how I would dispense my approval and disapproval and what the consequence of my disapproval would be. Would I strike back physically? Would I abandon her? Or, would I find a way to express my disapproval of her behavior without allowing the relationship to be destroyed?

Another part of this third phase of Alice's therapy was the increasing deterioration of her behavior in the milieu. Alice consistently continued to act verbally and often physically aggressively towards both her peers and the adult staff members. For example, Alice received psychiatric hospitalization three times in a two-month span because of her aggressive behaviors.

Following her return from the last hospitalization during that phase, I saw a marked decrease in the number of sessions she missed because she was with the crisis counselor. In addition, I also saw a decrease in her need to create an unpleasant interaction with me immediately prior to leaving session when our time together was up. Rather than pretend to be asleep, simply refuse to leave, or begin to act aggressively at the end of session, Alice began to express to me in words that she enjoyed our time together so much that she was always sad when our session ended. I told her that I, too, enjoyed our time together but that I also knew that we both had other important things to do and that I would be looking forward to our next session together. For example, Alice and I would spend the last 10 minutes or so of our sessions quietly playing cards. During one game that was very long, I commented that it might just be "the longest game ever" of its kind. Alice, in a tone mixed with understanding and sadness, noted that she and I could never have "the longest game ever," because our games always have to stop when our session time is up.

I also began to be aware that her oral cravings for nurturance and the accompanying persistent fears of my abandonment of her were starting to give way to control issues more commonly associated with what might be described as the anal phase of psychosexual development. This was expressed by our interactions around food. At an earlier point, Alice had asked me if I would get her a special candy jar for her to keep in my session room so that she could have a sweet treat during our sessions. That next day I purchased a small blue ceramic candy jar and some "treats" with which to stock it. I also told Alice, who was overweight, that there were a couple of conditions to this arrangement. The first was that she could only have a modest amount of candy at each session. The second was that she could not make the other children jealous by returning to her classroom after our sessions and gloating to the other children about the candy. Initially, this worked out well.

Alice soon began to try, however, to bargain different arrangements that would allow her to eat as much as possible. In spite of this almost constant bargaining for control of the candy jar, Alice seemed to continue to experience me as a "good object" and to become quite responsive to my attempts to set limits on her behavior when she was with me. For example, she would often follow my directions on our way to and from session and when becoming increasingly disruptive, a quick, stern word from me typically provided enough motivation for her to stop whatever it was that she should not have been doing.

In addition, Alice began to verbalize communications of her positive transferential feelings towards me within the therapeutic relationship. An example of one of her communications of the positive transference was the routine that she established with me for returning to her classroom following our sessions. My session room was on the third floor of the building, and in order to get to it Alice and I had to walk up many stairs. When we would return from session and walk down all those stairs, Alice would request that I go first, several steps ahead of her, so that she could place her hand on my shoulder as we walked down the steps. Initially, Alice asked to do this because she claimed to need to steady herself going down the stairs (no matter that there was a hand rail). One day when we were leaving session and after this had been going on for several weeks Alice asked me, "Do you like it when I put my hand on your shoulder when we walk down the steps?" I responded that I knew it was something that she did each time we walked down the steps after session and that I liked the fact that she and I had rituals that we shared together.

All of these interactions implied a certain tone to the therapeutic sessions that were in stark contrast to her behavior in other aspects of the milieu. Had I succeeded in positioning myself as one of Altman's (1995) "new objects" in Alice's internal object world? Around the same period of time, Alice had begun to talk with me about the troublesome incidents she was having more generally in the milieu. Although she would typically only give the basic facts of the incidents in ways that were at times truthful and at other times less accurate, she was always quite willing to discuss the incidents with me.

Also during this time period, Alice began to run away from the crisis counselors during these incidents to my office. If I were not there, she would sit outside the door awaiting my return; if I were there, she would "barge" into my office. She was often hyperventilating and quite obviously upset. At these times, I would remind Alice of the relaxation techniques that I had previously taught her (e.g., "belly breaths") and after she was physically calm I would call the main office to have them inform the crisis counselor that Alice was with me. Alice and I would then begin to talk whatever problem had occurred until the crisis counselor arrived at my office. We would continue to talk for several minutes after the counselor had arrived before they would return to the milieu together.

To give one specific example of this pattern, on the day of another student's graduation from the school, Alice awoke in the morning having wet her bed during the night. She was very upset, not to mention humiliated by this, but she was trying in spite of that episode to get dressed nicely for the graduation ceremony later in the day. However, she didn't have any dress shoes to wear and had asked to borrow a pair from another student. Although the school rules forbid borrowing, staff often allows children to borrow on special occasions. On this occasion, staff refused to allow it and this represented a big blow to Alice's attempts to get dressed nicely. Then, as she was trying to get her hair done nicely with a red hair tie that she had received as a prize for doing well the evening before, one of the other children in her dormitory threw the hair tie into the garbage. By then, it was breakfast time and in spite of her efforts to get dressed nicely and on time, Alice had made no progress: she had no nice shoes, her hair was a mess, and she was upset about both, as well as feeling humiliated by having wet the bed the previous evening.

When she saw me at breakfast, she could not contain herself and ran to me giving me a hug and complaining about how badly she felt. After consoling her briefly, I directed her to stay with her group and to try to enjoy breakfast. She managed to do so until her group finished eating, but as I was the only staff member at the staff table she walked by on her way out, she ran to me again, this time crying uncontrollably. I told her counselor that Alice could stay with me and talk while I finished eating. We discussed what had happened earlier in the morning, came up with alternative ways to look nice than with borrowed shoes and that particular hair tie, and I took her back to the dormitory and communicated the plan to her counselor. Less than 5 minutes later, Alice came running from the dormitory in tears searching for me because another of the students had spilled water (purposefully in Alice's opinion) on the socks that she and her counselor had picked out to go with her outfit. I found her (waiting for me outside my office), helped her calm down, and explained the situation to the crisis counselor who helped her finish getting ready for the day by combing her hair and picking out new socks.

Milieu staff perceptions, however, were that Alice continued to struggle. Her problems in the classroom persisted, as did her problems in the dormitory. In session, Alice and I continued to maintain a positive therapeutic relationship. We would talk about incidents in which she had been involved, as well as about other concerns of hers mostly related to the daily happenings at the school. Problems in the milieu had begun to include allegations by other students that Alice was "touching" inappropriately, and because Alice had a history of such behavior, a formal investigation was launched. The milieu continued to be unstable for her both because of Alice's behavior and because of chronic turnover in direct-care staff.

Also during this time period, Alice's biological father entered the scene. Living in another state, he and his wife began visiting Alice and expressing an interest in becoming formally involved with her case. Although the travel distance presented the family with some difficulty in visiting Alice, they appeared to be a consistent visiting resource for her. Nevertheless, Alice's behavior continued to be severely problematic, and when she was hospitalized yet another time for rageful, physically aggressive behaviors, she was discharged to a more structured residential setting than the school could provide.

COUNTERTRANSFERENCE IN TREATMENT WITH CHILDREN AND ADOLESCENTS

One difficulty with the literature about countertransference is a certain amount of ambiguity about the definition of the concept. Classically, countertransference is the transfer of feelings from the therapist's past onto the patient (usually, but not necessarily, in response to the patient's transference). In this sense, countertransference was regarded as a hindrance to the therapy process because the therapist was supposed to remain a neutral interpreter of the patient's experience. More recently, the concept has both been broadened to include the total emotional reaction of the therapist to the patient (Hoffman, 1998) and extended, by the shift from a one-person framework to two- and three-person frameworks, to be considered one of, if not the most, critical element of the therapy process (Mitchell & Black, 1995).

According to Mitchell and Black (1995), Ferenczi, Racker, and Sullivan and the other interpersonalists were the pioneers of the new approach to countertransference and of the two-person frameworks of the therapeutic situation. In short, and drawing heavily upon Sullivan, a two-person framework acknowledges that the patient is part of an interactive field made up of many individuals. For Sullivan, it is difficult, if not impossible, to consider the individual patient apart from that context. Ferenczi and Racker extended Sullivan's interactive field theory by acknowledging that the analyst, too, is part of that interactive field. The significance of these observations is that they represent the origins of countertransference being thought of as a way of understanding the patient and as a critical part of the therapeutic work.

Three-person frameworks of the therapeutic situation (Altman, 1995; Hoffman, 1998; Altman et al., 2002) extend the two-person frameworks by extending the field to include the context within which the psychotherapeutic relationship occurs. Altman (1995) discusses some of the ways in which that context comes into play for therapists working within the inner-city clinic. For example, the therapist in such a clinic is often in the role of being a provider of snacks or of transportation funds. Those roles typically involve one to take a more active stance than a therapist may otherwise choose to take and carry over into the therapeutic relationship during the therapy hour in a manner that is not always straightforward.

Altman et al. (2002) apply three-person perspectives to directly to work with children. As it applies to work with children, the field theory approach includes not only the child and his/her therapist, but also the parents, families, teachers, tutors, and other professionals with whom the child comes into contact. The authors note that "child therapists who keep an eye on the various systems that interface with the child may feel inclined to take a relatively interventionist approach to the work. They are also likely to feel quite overwhelmed by the number of things that need to be attended to" (p. 285). The feeling of being overwhelmed is just one type of countertransference feeling that therapists may experience.

There is very little literature that deals directly with the issues of transference and countertransference in the residential treatment of severely emotionally disturbed children and adolescents (cf., Borowitz, 1970). Halperin et al. (1981) discussed the issue of countertransference in the context of a long-term transitional residential treatment program for troubled adolescents. They noted that the countertransference implications of certain program rules, such as that of mandatory attendance at individual psychotherapy sessions, are profound. For example, the therapist may resent being placed in a role that requires them to coerce their patients to attend sessions by either adopting rigid expectations of attendance that ally him/her with the institution against the patient, or by acting "out his frustration and countertransference by aligning himself with the resident" against the institution (p. 560).

Writing about countertransference in therapy with children and adolescents generally, Marshall (1979) suggested that the feelings can be more intense than in work with adults. Masterson (1972), in his writing about therapy with borderline adolescents, addressed the therapist's management of countertransference in each of three phases of the therapy process. In the first, the testing phase, he notes that the countertransference problems "involve the task of being firm, consistent, and assertive in the face of acting out" (Halperin et al., 1981, p. 563). In the second phase, that of working-through, the countertransference difficulty may be "reflected in the therapist's ability to tolerate intense affect in the form of hostility or depression" (Halperin et al., 1981, p. 563). In the final, termination phase, the countertransference problem for the therapist is that of not pushing the patient too strongly towards independence and autonomy.

In writing specifically about countertransference in residential treatment of children and adolescents, Halperin et al. (1981) discussed that the long-term nature of their program made the general therapeutic situation ripe for rescue fantasies and that the residential staff could retaliate by behaving aggressively towards the adolescents when they resist rescue. The authors also noted that the residential treatment setting also presents the dilemma of countertransference feelings among staff in the general milieu. They argue that the different roles staff members play foster countertransference splitting. The direct-care staff, who must enforce rules, are often subject to the patient's hostility and negative transferences. They may envy the more likely positive transferences that the therapist role engenders and may unconsciously work to sabotage the patient's progress. Conversely, the therapist may envy the quality of the more ongoing relationships that direct-care staff members develop with the adolescents.

There is also some writing on how collective staff countertransference affects the general treatment effort within a therapeutic community, or residential treatment setting. Stanton and Schwartz (1954) showed that unbridled staff countertransference reactions significantly impact a patient's symptoms for the worse. Adler (1973) noted that staff with differing roles often argue about whose vision of the patient is the more correct. King (1976) commented how personal staff countertransference reactions to acting out can range from appeasement to identification (both of which are problematic in their own right).

Cohen (1988), in his writing about residential treatment with abused children and adolescents, discusses what he calls the "golden fantasy." This fantasy is the abused child's wish to have her needs perfectly met through no work of her own. According to Cohen, it is the child's placement in a residential treatment setting, where basic needs are met and where she is no longer a victim of abuse, which evokes the "golden fantasy." The direct-care staff members, however, devote themselves "completely to the child's needs to the point where his[/her] own golden fantasy is evoked. Through countertransference and projective identification, he fulfills it through the child he is treating. By means of different processes, especially the mechanism of splitting, the parents are perceived as evil creatures to be avoided, as opposed to the benevolent and omnipotent therapists" (p. 338). After some time, however, and "again by means of the mechanism of splitting, the child perceives his care workers as the evil persons who do not fulfill his golden fantasy (and this fantasy functions on an 'all or nothing' basis). He again turns to his parents and attributes to them the ability to fulfill his fantasy. The therapist who devoted his entire self to the abused child is disappointed and in despair. Through projective identification the child succeeds in bringing the therapist to fulfill the role of the abusing parent, even though the therapist refrains from any physical abuse" (p. 338).

In some of the only presentations of failures in residential treatment with emotionally disturbed children and adolescents, Eckstein, Wallerstein, and Mandelbaum (1966, 1992) discussed countertransference patterns among staff at the Southard School of the Menninger Clinic. Eckstein et al. described staff rescue fantasies and the accompanying frustration and anger that appeared when their efforts did not bring about the changes and progress in the child about which they were fantasizing. As they discuss, staff members' anger and frustration, which was initially directed towards the children's abusive parents or other obviously "bad objects," came to be directed towards the supervisory staff, the therapist, or, when the treatments really fail, onto the child him- or herself.

In summary, and from the vantage of the direct-care worker, negative countertransference feelings are evoked in the worker as a result of his/her difficult work with the child. The worker, in an attempt to avoid dealing with those at times overwhelmingly negative feelings, projects them onto the child, the child's parents, and the child's therapist. But the worker identifies with those feelings in a modified way; the projection cannot be complete because the feelings are, after all, the worker's feelings. As the child always experiences some continuation of his/her difficulties, the child, his/her parents, and his/her therapist are all inevitably viewed in negative terms by the direct-care worker. It is far easier, after all, to blame others for problems than it is to look at those aspects of one's own behavior with respect to the child that may, in fact, be less than adequate. It should be noted that the same processes at play for the direct-care worker are also at play for the child, the parents, and the therapist. It is in the interests of brevity that I have restricted my discussions of these processes to focus on the direct-care worker.

COUNTERTRANSFERENCE IN THE TREATMENT OF ALICE

Many of the observations contained in the writings about countertransference in work with children and adolescents generally, and in residential settings in particular, have obvious parallels to Alice's case. For one, Masterson's (1972) discussion of the different countertransference reactions to be expected at each of the different phases of the individual therapy process resonates with my conceptualization of the phases of my work with Alice. Although my work with Alice seemed to have vacillated between the testing phase and the working-through phase, the initial phase of my work with Alice was definitely one in which she tested limits and in which the countertransference-related struggles for me were both in being strict enough to enforce limits versus being nurturing, and in dealing with feelings of inadequacy and incompetence when she failed to adhere to the limits I set. This was particularly true during the period of time in which Alice was refusing to leave after our sessions together.

The discussion of Halperin et al. (1981) of how the different roles of residential workers create the possibility for countertransference splitting also applies to my therapy with Alice. Alice behaved in general so differently with me than she did in other aspects of the milieu that at different points in the therapy process I was convinced that the residential and classroom staff were unresponsive to Alice's needs. Although I attempted to readily acknowledge that I had the luxury of interacting with Alice on a one-to-one basis, I harbored large amounts of animosity, particularly towards the residential staff, for what I felt was their inability to meet Alice's needs. I was, however, very seldom in that role and when I was in that role, I did not also have the responsibility of managing the behavior of several other children and adolescents.

Perhaps the most interesting issue, however, is that of how staff, myself included, became frustrated and angry at our inability to rescue Alice from her situation. In retrospect I imagine that we all harbored fantasies of bringing about miraculous changes in Alice's behavior. When those changes did not occur, the feelings that Alice evoked in the countertransferences with all of us were not adequately dealt with. For me, the frustration was displaced in a manner similar to that discussed by Cohen (1988) and Eckstein et al. (1992), onto other staff at the school. For the residential staff, classroom teachers, and crisis counselors, however, the displacement was to Alice. By the time of her discharge, staff members were acting on their negative countertransference feelings towards Alice.

DISCUSSION

This paper presented selected aspects of a psychodynamic psychotherapy with a highly depressed and aggressive young girl in residential care. Her early life was profoundly influenced by multiple caregiver rejections and abandonment, as well as by possible experiences of physical and sexual abuse. Upon admission to the residential setting, her emotional and behavioral difficulties were severe.

The case material has been used to illustrate the issues of transference and countertransference as they apply to the individual psychotherapy of a child in residential treatment. Although the literature on transference and countertransference in residential treatment typically takes a broad definition, it also generally reflects one- and two-person frameworks of the therapeutic situation. That may be especially problematic for the residential treatment of children and adolescents where staff members, like those in Altman's (1995) inner-city clinic, must necessarily fill multiple roles for the patient when the larger contexts of the child's life and residential milieu are considered.

A three-person framework has been quite helpful in my attempts to understand therapeutic work with severely emotionally disturbed children and adolescents in a residential treatment setting. The larger context within which an individual therapy with a severely emotionally disturbed child in residential treatment occurs is so unusually intense that it permeates the walls of the session room in ways that go beyond issues traditionally related to transference and countertransference. As countertransference goes, however, I hope that this case of a residential treatment and individual therapy failure suggest the negative impact that unrecognized countertransference may have on a patient's capacity to experience enhanced psychological growth.

Zimmerman (1999) has commented that the call for a more limited use of residential treatment may in and of itself reflect the presence of unusually intense transference and countertransference reactions towards residential institutions. It may also be that providing residential treatment services in the context of the collusion between scientism and concerns for fiscal responsibility (Zimmerman, 2000) has produced models of residential care that are even less able to deal with the difficult countertransference reactions that arise in work with severely emotionally disturbed children and adolescents.

NOTES

1. The student's name has been changed to preserve anonymity.
2. Clinical supervision for the individual therapy case was provided by D. Patrick Zimmerman, PsyD.

REFERENCES

Adler, G. (1973). Hospital treatment of borderline patients. *American Journal of Psychiatry*, 1, pp. 25-32.

Ainsworth, M.D.S. (1973). The development of infant-mother attachment. In B.M. Caldwell & H.N. Ricciuti (Eds.), *Review of child development research*. Vol. 3. pp. 1-94. Chicago: University of Chicago Press.

Altman, N. (1995). *The analyst in the inner city: Race, class, and culture through a psychoanalytic lens*. Hillsdale, NJ: The Analytic Press.

Altman, N., Briggs, R., Frankel, J., Gensler, D., & Pantone, P. (2002). *Relational child psychotherapy*. New York: Other Press.

American Psychiatric Association. (1994). *Diagnostic and statistical manual of mental disorders* (4th ed. rev.). Washington, DC: American Psychiatric Press.

Bettelheim, B. (1950). *Love is not enough*. New York: Free Press.

Bettelheim, B. (1955). *Truants from life*. New York: Free Press.

Bettelheim, B. (1967). *The empty fortress*. New York: Free Press.

Bettelheim, B. (1974). *A home for the heart*. New York: Knopf.

Bettelheim, B., & Sylvester, E. (1947). Therapeutic influence of the group on the individual. *American Journal of Orthopsychiatry*, 17, pp. 684-692.

Bettelheim, B., & Sylvester, E. (1948). A therapeutic milieu. *American Journal of Orthopsychiatry*, 18, pp. 191-206.

Borowitz, G.H. (1970). The therapeutic utilization of emotions and attitudes evoked in the caretakers of disturbed children. *British Journal of Medical Psychology*, 43, 129-139.

Bowlby, J. (1969). *Attachment and loss, Vol. 1: Attachment*. London: Pimlico.

Brandell, J.R. (1992). *Countertransference in psychotherapy with children & adolescents*. Northvale, New Jersey: Jason Aronson, Inc.

Children's Defense Fund. (1997). *The state of America's children: Yearbook 1997.* Washington, DC: Children's Defense Fund.

Cohen, Y. (1988). The "golden fantasy" and countertransference: Residential treatment of the abused child. *Psychoanalytic Study of the Child*, 43, pp. 337-350.

Ekstein, R., Wallerstein, J., & Mendelbaum, A. (1992). Countertransference in the residential treatment of children. In J.R. Brandell (Ed.), *Countertransference in psychotherapy with children & adolescents.* Northvale, New Jersey: Jason Aronson, Inc.

Eisikovitis, R.A., & Schwartz, I.M. (1991). The future of residential education and care. *Residential Treatment for Children & Youth*, 8(3), pp. 5-19.

Epstein, L., & Feiner, A.H., (Eds.). (1979). Countertransference. New York: Jason Aronson, Inc.

Gaensbauer, T.J. (2000). Psychotherapeutic treatment of traumatized infants and toddlers. *Clinical Child Psychology and Psychiatry*, 5(3), pp. 373-385.

Gil, E. (1991). *The healing power of play: Working with abused children.* London: Guilford Press.

Halperin, D., Lauro, G., Miscione, F., Rebhan, J., Schnabolk, J., & Shachter, B. (1981). Countertransference issues in a transitional residential treatment program for troubled adolescents. *Adolescent Psychiatry*, 9, pp. 559-577.

Hoffman, I.Z. (1998). *Ritual and spontaneity in the psychoanalytic process: A dialectical-constructivist view.* Hillsdale, NJ: The Analytic Press.

King, C. (1976). Countertransference and counterexperience in the treatment of violence prone youth. *American Journal of Orthopsychiatry*, 46, pp. 43-52.

Levy, T., & Orlans, M. (1995). Intensive short-term therapy with attachment disordered children. In L. VandeCreek, S. Knapp, & T.L. Jackson (Eds.), *Innovations in clinical practice: A sourcebook. Vol. 14.* pp. 227-251. Sarasota, FL: Professional Resource Press.

Levy, T. & Orlans, M. (1998). *Attachment, trauma and healing.* Washington, DC: Child Welfare League of America Press.

Levy, T., (Ed.). (2000). *Handbook of attachment interventions.* San Diego: Academic Press.

Marshall, R.J. (1979). Countertransference with children and adolescents. In L. Epstein & A.H. Feiner (Eds.), *Countertransference.* New York: Jason Aronson, Inc.

Marvasti, T. (1993). 'Please hurt me again': Posttraumatic play therapy with an abused child. In T. Kottman & C.E. Schaefer (Eds.), *Play therapy in action.* pp. 485-525. Norvthvale, New Jersey: Jason Aronson, Inc.

Masterson, J.F. (1972). *Treatment of the borderline adolescents: A developmental approach.* New York: Wiley.

Mitchell, S.A., & Black, M.J. (1995). *Freud and beyond: A history of modern psychoanalytic thought.* New York: Basic Books.

Ofosky, J.D. (1995). The effects of exposure to violence on young children. *American Psychologist*, 50, pp. 782-788.

Ogden, T.H. (1982). *Projective identification and psychotherapeutic technique.* New York: Jason Aronson.

Sanders, J. (1989). *A greenhouse for the mind.* Chicago: University of Chicago Press.

Schaefer, C.E. (1994). Play therapy for psychic trauma in children. In K.J. O'Connor & C.E. Schaefer (Eds.), *Handbook of play therapy. Vol. II.* pp. 297-318. Chichester, UK: Wiley.

Shelby, J.S. (2000). Brief therapy with traumatized children: A developmental perspective. In H.G. Kaduson & C.E. Schaefer (Eds.), *Short-term play therapy for children.* pp. 69-104. London: Guilford.

Stanton, A.H., & Schwartz, M.S. (1954). *The mental hospital.* New York: Basic Books.

Zimmerman, D.P. (1990). Notes on the history of adolescent inpatient and residential treatment. *Adolescence,* 25, pp. 9-38.

Zimmerman, D.P. (1994). A pilot demographic study of population changes in a residential treatment center. *Residential Treatment for Children and Youth,* 11(3), 17-33.

Zimmerman, D.P. (1999). Desperation and hope in the analysis of a "thrown-away" adolescent boy. *Psychoanalytic Psychology,* 16(2), pp. 198-232.

Zimmerman, D.P. (2000). Psychotherapy in residential treatment: The human toll of scientism and managed care. *Residential Treatment for Children and Youth,* 18(2), pp. 55-86.

Zimmerman, D.P. (2000). *The forsaken child: Essays on group care and individual therapy.* New York: Haworth Press, Inc.

Zimmerman, D.P., & Cohler, B.J. (1998). From disciplinary control to benign milieu in children's residential treatment. *Therapeutic Communities,* 19, pp. 123-147.

BIOGRAPHICAL NOTE

Richard A. Epstein, Jr., MA, received his master's degree from and is currently a doctoral candidate in the Committee on Human Development in the Department of Psychology at the University of Chicago. He is a Program Manager at the Sonia Shankman Orthogenic School at the University of Chicago and Managing Editor of *Residential Treatment for Children & Youth.*

The Integration of Psychotherapy and Residential Treatment in an Intensive Short-Term Treatment Program: Part I. Structural Considerations

Martin Leichtman, PhD
Maria Luisa Leichtman, PhD

SUMMARY. This paper examines the structural basis for the integration of psychotherapy and residential treatment by considering: (1) what is meant by integration; (2) variables bearing on the manner and degree to which it can be accomplished; and (3) changes in the roles of psychotherapists that maximize each of those variables. Subsequent papers will consider ways in which approaches to psychotherapy can be adapted to the altered forms of clinical practice these changes entail and specific ways in which that integration was accomplished in each phase of the treatment process. *[Article copies available for a fee from The Haworth Document Delivery Service: 1-800-HAWORTH. E-mail address: <docdelivery@haworthpress.com> Website: <http://www.HaworthPress.com> © 2003 by The Haworth Press, Inc. All rights reserved.]*

The authors may be written at: The Foxhill Medical Building, 4601 West 109th Street–Suite 240, Overland Park, KS 66211.

[Haworth co-indexing entry note]: "The Integration of Psychotherapy and Residential Treatment in an Intensive Short-Term Treatment Program: Part I. Structural Considerations." Leichtman, Martin, and Maria Luisa Leichtman. Co-published simultaneously in *Residential Treatment for Children & Youth* (The Haworth Press, Inc.) Vol. 20, No. 4, 2003, pp. 73-80; and: *Psychotherapy in Group Care: Making Life Good Enough* (ed: D. Patrick Zimmerman et al.) The Haworth Press, Inc., 2003, pp. 73-80. Single or multiple copies of this article are available for a fee from The Haworth Document Delivery Service [1-800-HAWORTH, 9:00 a.m. - 5:00 p.m. (EST). E-mail address: docdelivery@haworthpress.com].

10.1300/J007v20n04_05

KEYWORDS. Short-term residential treatment, therapist-resident interactions, psychotherapy and residential treatment, integration of treatment processes, psychotherapy process

In recent papers, we described a model of intensive short-term residential treatment for severely disturbed adolescents and follow-up data on its effectiveness (Leichtman & Leichtman, 1996a, 1996b, 1996c; Leichtman, Leichtman, Barber, & Neese, 2001). The term "intensive" was used to denote that the model was developed to provide services comparable to those of intermediate- and long-term psychiatric hospitals that were no longer readily available after the managed care revolution of the early 1990s. That is to say, the program (1) was intended for adolescents with psychoses, serious character pathology, and marked anxiety and affective disorders whose self-injurious acting-out, incapacitating symptoms, and failure to negotiate social and adaptational tasks could not be managed through comprehensive outpatient treatment and/or brief hospitalizations, and (2) included the same basic services (e.g., a structured, carefully supervised milieu, medication, psychotherapy, group therapy, family therapy, and specialized treatments for substance abuse, eating problems, and trauma) formerly offered in those hospitals.

The model was "residential" in the sense that it was organized around principles that distinguish that modality from other forms of inpatient treatment. It was based on the assumptions that: (1) to address severe psychopathology, it is essential to help children negotiate basic tasks of daily living effectively; (2) such treatment requires a coordinated team, each of whose members work on common therapeutic issues in their own ways; (3) the central agents of change are the caretakers, the childcare staff, who are most directly involved in this process; and (4) all other aspects of treatment must be organized around and fed into the work of the residential unit. The model was "short-term" not only in the sense that typical lengths of stay were 3 to 4 months, far less than those characteristic of traditional residential programs, but also that treatment was based on principles common to short-term therapies of all kinds (Budman & Gurman, 1988; Leichtman & Leichtman, 1996b).

An essential feature of this program was the rigorous integration of psychotherapy with other aspects of residential treatment, especially the work of the childcare staff. This paper examines the structural basis for this process by considering: (1) what is meant by integration; (2) variables bearing on the manner and degree to which it can be accomplished; and (3) changes in the roles of psychotherapists that maximize each of those variables. Subsequent papers will consider ways in which approaches to psychotherapy can be adapted to the altered forms of clinical practice these changes entail and specific ways in which that integration was accomplished in each phase of the treatment process.

THERAPIST-RESIDENCE INTERACTIONS

What is described as the integration of the psychotherapy and residential treatment may involve a wide range of interactions between team members. A good point of departure for understanding them is a consideration of what therapists and unit staff may seek from one another.

Therapists usually wish three types of assistance from childcare workers that are similar to those from parents in outpatient psychotherapy processes. *First*, they are dependent on the residential unit, as they are on parents, for such basic support as getting children to therapy on time, conveying a sense of its importance, and dealing with children's resistance to the process during difficult periods when they may not make use of therapy or even balk at coming to it. *Second*, therapists typically would like caretakers to provide information about children's behavior, the circumstances of their day-to-day lives, and environmental factors impinging on them. Such information may help determine problems to be worked on in therapy, establish a context for understanding material arising in sessions, and serve as a means of assessing whether children are improving or not. *Third*, as therapists learn about factors in children's lives that contribute to problems or inhibit their growth, they may wish parents or caretakers to make changes in the environment or alter patterns of interaction within the family. At times, therapists go farther and use caretakers as their surrogates in such tasks as helping children face anxiety-arousing situations or providing coaching and assistance in controlling aggression or improving relationships with siblings or peers.

What unit staff need from therapists may be understood in terms of two basic assumptions about what is curative in residential treatment. One, implicit in the concepts of the therapeutic milieu and "the other 23 hours" (Trieschman, Whittaker, & Brendtro, 1969), is that whatever is done to enable troubled children to negotiate basic tasks of daily living (waking, grooming, eating, school, recreation, relations with caretakers and peers, etc.) is in innumerable small, but cumulatively large, ways treating the anxiety, depression, aggression, thought disorder, or other types of psychopathology that have disrupted their lives and that, even if such interventions cannot eliminate symptoms entirely, they can provide children with the adaptive skills to live satisfying lives in spite of their problems. Childcare staff, who are chiefly responsible for this aspect of treatment, often wish that therapists would assist them by making these issues a major focus of the psychotherapy process as well and by providing extensive consultation to help them deal with pathology that interferes with children managing these tasks.

The other assumption that distinguishes residential treatment as a modality, that embodied in the concept of the "life space interview" (Redl, 1966), is that symptoms are best addressed while they are occurring or shortly afterward. If therapy could be conducted at these times, the events leading to problems and their sequence would be fresh in everyone's minds and have affective resonance as they may not in the next formal psychotherapy session several days later; children's defenses are down; and therapists can apply "emotional first aid" to prevent symptoms from mushrooming into full-fledged crises. Such interviews often cannot be conducted by psychotherapists, who cannot be on residential units 24 hours a day, but they are possible if the staff who are with children at these times perform these functions as well. Hence, in so far as they conduct such "life space interviews," childcare workers may wish therapists to accept the sharing of the psychotherapy role, supply information about children's conflicts and dynamics to enable workers to conduct such interviews better, and offer guidance and even supervision in doing so.

VARIABLES BEARING ON THE INTEGRATION
OF PSYCHOTHERAPY AND RESIDENTIAL PROGRAMS

Because the integration of psychotherapy and residential treatment may involve a variety of interactions between therapists and the residential unit, the manner and extent to which it takes place in any given program varies considerably. Moreover, because therapists and unit staff within the same program have their own distinct perspectives and priorities, each may prefer types of interactions, and the very meaning of "integration" may differ for each. Consequently, how and to what degree psychotherapy and residential treatment are integrated is determined by a number of variables.

One is the treatment philosophies that govern each process. As a rule, therapists prefer to work with residential staff in the same ways they do with parents in outpatient processes. For example, some psychotherapists (e.g., Axline, 1969; Glenn, 1978; Weiss, 1964) focus chiefly on events within the session itself and limit communication with caretakers. Others, such as many psychoanalytically-oriented therapists, may seek information about children's lives and provide feedback to caretakers, but do so in controlled, delimited ways intended to preserve confidentiality and maintain the boundaries of the therapy relationship (e.g., Coppolillo, 1987). Still other therapists welcome as much sharing of information and consultation as possible. The degree of integration may also vary with the cases treated. As a rule, therapists favor more extensive and more candid interchanges around younger and more disturbed clients than around older and more intact ones. Similarly, residential programs differ in how much and what kind of input they seek from therapists. Typically, they are likely to want more extensive information and consultation than therapists. However, some may be most comfortable with keeping the two types of treatment processes separate because of set residential treatment protocols, concerns that too much consultation from therapists can confuse and disrupt treatment on the units (especially if there are several therapists with different orientations), or practical considerations such as cost and logistics.

A closely related factor is the treatment philosophy that governs the residential system as a whole. Systems differ in the degree to which integration is valued (Monahan, 1989). As noted, some are content with both processes being discrete or with limited interchange either for theoretical reasons (e.g., concerns about preserving the integrity of each treatment process) or because of the time, expense, and energy involved in doing otherwise. Others expect extensive contact between therapists and the residence. The overriding philosophies also determine who sets the terms of integration when there are differences between the residence and therapists. For example, in a number of early programs, psychoanalysis and psychotherapy were viewed as the preeminent component of treatment. The residence was to provide a benign living environment while the primary therapeutic work occurred in an intensive psychotherapy process. Therapists thus might receive more information from the residential team than they returned and could expect their recommendations regarding children's needs on the unit to be put into practice. In contrast, over the years, work on the residence assumed increasing importance and in many programs psychotherapy came to be considered only one of a number of concurrent treatments. In such programs, there might be tolerance for treating each process as separate or therapists might be expected to integrate their work on the residence's terms, with referrals and even employment being contingent upon their willingness to accept those terms.

Another variable is the status of psychotherapists in the residential system. In programs in which psychotherapy was conducted by psychoanalysts or other experienced, highly-trained clinicians, therapists could expect their requests for information to be taken seriously and for their recommendations to have a significant impact on the residential treatment process. In contrast, in programs in which psychotherapy is conducted by less sophisticated clinicians with relatively modest credentials, the views of therapists carry less weight with the residential team. All other things being equal, the greater the power and authority of the psychotherapist, the greater the degree to which the psychotherapy process may influence residential treatment.

All other things are seldom equal, however. For example, even if the word of a psychoanalyst consulting to a residential team is accorded the authority of the Holy Writ, ordinary mortals on the unit might be limited in their understanding of the therapist's intent or even take a sinful pleasure in ignoring it, especially if the therapist is viewed as an outsider. Therapy is more likely to be coordinated with the work of the rest of the residential program when therapists are viewed as integral parts of the residential team than when they are seen as peripheral or not part of the team at all.

Finally, even when the administration, therapist, and unit staff wish for a high degree of integration of treatment processes, the extent to which it actually occurs depends on communication within the team. Such communication may be affected by geography (e.g., whether therapists' offices are on or near the unit or whether they are off the service or even outside the institution), the frequency of meetings and their agendas, and time demands on staff (e.g., whether there are opportunities for informal exchange of information). Obviously, programs with regular meetings attended by therapists, ones in which therapists are on the unit often, and ones in which staff can exchange information frequently in both formal and informal ways are more likely to coordinate the two types of treatment processes than ones in which there is limited and infrequent contact.

THE ROLE OF THE PRIMARY CLINICIAN AND THE INTEGRATION OF TREATMENT PROCESSES

Assuming that a high degree of synthesis is necessary in order to handle diminished lengths of stay and make comprehensive treatment economical, intensive, short-term residential treatment places a premium on the integration of psychotherapy and all other aspects of treatment. The critical step in translating that philosophy into practice lay in a fundamental structural change in the role and functions of psychotherapists on the unit.

That change consisted of the adoption of a variation of the combined therapist-administrator model (Monahan, 1989). A single individual, a "primary clinician," was given responsibility for providing diagnosis, treatment planning, team leadership, psychotherapy, and group therapy for a number of adolescents on the unit (Leichtman & Leichtman, 1996c). In effect, the roles of team leader, psychotherapist, and group therapist for children were combined.

The significance of this redefinition of roles lies in the fact that it maximizes each of the variables contributing to the integration of psychotherapy and residential treatment. The treatment philosophy permeating the residential program obviously makes such integration a central value. Psychotherapists, by virtue of also directing the residential program for a child, have a high status in the system and authority for decision-making. Far from being "outsiders," primary clinicians occupy a central role in the residential team. And, since they are present at most key meetings and have numerous formal and informal contacts with staff on the residential unit daily, they are in constant communication with other members of the team and can have input into decisions about even relatively minor aspects of treatment.

In sum, the primary clinician model is one in which the potential for bringing issues on the unit into the psychotherapy process and for translating insights from the psychotherapy process into unit treatment could hardly be greater.

REFERENCES

Axline, V. M. (1969). *Play therapy.* New York: Ballantine.

Bettelheim, B. & Sanders, J. (1979). Milieu therapy: The Orthogenic School model. In J. A. Noshpitz (Ed.), *Basic handbook of child psychiatry: Vol. 3. Therapeutic interventions* (pp. 216-230). New York: Basic Books.

Coppolillo, H. P. (1987). *Psychodynamic psychotherapy with children: An introduction to the art and the technique.* Madison, CT: International Universities Press.

Glenn, J. (1978). General principles of child analysis. In J. Glenn (Ed.), *Child analysis and therapy* (pp. 29-64). New York: Jason Aronson.

Leichtman, M. & Leichtman, M. L. (1996a). A model of short-term residential treatment: I. The nature of the challenge. In C. Waller (Ed.), *Contributions to residential treatment 1996* (pp. 85-92). Alexandria, VA: American Association of Children's Residential Centers.

Leichtman, M. & Leichtman, M. L. (1996b). A model of short-term residential treatment: II. General principles. In C. Waller (Ed.), *Contributions to residential treatment 1996* (pp. 93-102). Alexandria, VA: American Association of Children's Residential Centers.

Leichtman, M. & Leichtman, M. L. (1996c). A model of short-term residential treatment: III. Changing roles. In C. Waller (Ed.), *Contributions to residential treatment 1996* (pp. 103-109). Alexandria, VA: American Association of Children's Residential Centers.

Leichtman, M., Leichtman, M. L., Barber, C. B., & Neese, D. T. (2001). Effectiveness of intensive short-term residential treatment with severely disturbed adolescents. *American Journal of Orthopsychiatry, 71,* 227-235.

Monahan, R. T. (1989). Individual and group psychotherapy. In R. D. Lyman, S. Prentice-Dunn, & S. Gabel (Eds.), *Residential and inpatient treatment of children and adolescents* (pp. 191-205). New York: Plenum Press.

Redl, F. (1966). *When we deal with children.* New York: Free Press.

Redl, F. & Wineman, D. (1957). *The aggressive child.* Glencoe, IL: The Free Press.

Stone, L. A. (1979). Residential treatment. In J. A. Noshpitz (Ed.), *Basic handbook of child psychiatry: Vol. 3. Therapeutic interventions* (pp. 231-262). New York: Basic Books.
Trieschman, A. E., Whittaker, J. K., & Brendtro, L. K. (1969). *The other 23 hours.* Chicago: Aldine Publishing Company.
Weiss, S. (1964). Parameters in child analysis. *Journal of the American Psychoanalytic Association, 12,* 587-599.

BIOGRAPHICAL NOTES

Martin Leichtman, PhD, directed a residential treatment unit in the Child and Adolescent Unit of the Menninger Clinic and has served on the faculties of the Karl Menninger School of Mental Health Services and the Topeka Institute for Psychoanalysis.

Maria Luisa Leichtman, PhD, has served as Director of Residential Treatment at the Menninger Clinic.

The Integration of Psychotherapy and Residential Treatment in an Intensive Short-Term Treatment Program: Part II. Theoretical Considerations

Martin Leichtman, PhD
Maria Luisa Leichtman, PhD

SUMMARY. This paper will examine three sets of theoretical issues facing clinicians as they play multiple roles in short-term residential treatment. It will consider how potential conflicts in the roles of therapist and team leader can be resolved, the implications of such a resolution for the concept of confidentiality, and ways in which major approaches to psychotherapy can be adapted to new conditions. *[Article copies available for a fee from The Haworth Document Delivery Service: 1-800-HAWORTH. E-mail address: <docdelivery@haworthpress.com> Website: <http://www. HaworthPress.com> © 2003 by The Haworth Press, Inc. All rights reserved.]*

KEYWORDS. Brief psychotherapy, supportive psychotherapy, expressive psychotherapy, behavior and cognitive behavior therapy, short-term residential treatment

---

The authors may be written at: The Foxhill Medical Building, 4601 West 109th Street–Suite 240, Overland Park, KS 66211.

[Haworth co-indexing entry note]: "The Integration of Psychotherapy and Residential Treatment in an Intensive Short-Term Treatment Program: Part II. Theoretical Considerations." Leichtman, Martin, and Maria Luisa Leichtman. Co-published simultaneously in *Residential Treatment for Children & Youth* (The Haworth Press, Inc.) Vol. 20, No. 4, 2003, pp. 81-93; and: *Psychotherapy in Group Care: Making Life Good Enough* (ed: D. Patrick Zimmerman et al.) The Haworth Press, Inc., 2003, pp. 81-93. Single or multiple copies of this article are available for a fee from The Haworth Document Delivery Service [1-800-HAWORTH, 9:00 a.m. - 5:00 p.m. (EST). E-mail address: docdelivery@haworthpress.com].

10.1300/J007v20n04_06

INTRODUCTION

The preceding paper examined how adoption of a primary clinician model in which psychotherapists also direct teams provides the foundation for an extraordinary degree of integration of psychotherapy and residential treatment. However, as with any "reforms," alterations of the conditions in which psychotherapy is practiced can have a host of unintended consequences. Hence, the fact that such integration is possible does not necessarily mean that it is good for either psychotherapy or residential treatment.

When a single clinician plays many different roles, opportunities for feedback from a variety of sources are limited and fewer perspectives can be brought on treatment. More importantly, one role may interfere with the performance of others (Monahan, 1989; Stamm, 1989). And, above all, there is a danger that the boundaries that provide a framework for psychotherapy may become so permeable that the treatment process is undermined. For example, difficulties around maintenance of confidentiality, already problematic whenever therapists consult to treatment teams, are multiplied many times over for primary clinicians who are constantly involved in directing the treatment team. Understanding and working with transference becomes more difficult when outside influences on the therapy process are not controlled, but rather patients have numerous other contacts with therapists who make major decisions about their lives and have multiple relationships with significant figures in their environment. Similarly, countertransference reactions can no longer be read in terms of therapists' relationship with adolescents in the therapy hour alone, but are now affected by a host of other interactions outside of the therapy sessions as well as the reactions of other members of the treatment team to the patients. In such circumstances, even experienced clinicians assuming the role of primary clinician may well fear that rules that provide coherence for therapy processes have become fluid and that they are venturing into uncharted areas without guidance.

This paper will examine three sets of theoretical issues facing clinicians as they play multiple roles in short-term residential treatment. It will consider how potential conflicts in the roles of therapist and team leader can be resolved, the implications of such a resolution for the concept of confidentiality, and ways in which major approaches to psychotherapy can be adapted to new conditions.

PSYCHOTHERAPY AND THE PRIMACY OF RESIDENTIAL TREATMENT

Psychotherapy and residential treatment differ in certain fundamental respects. The former has traditionally been a centripetal process. In order to apply psychotherapeutic techniques in consistent ways and help patients share their most sensitive thoughts and feelings, therapists typically try to maintain the boundaries of the treatment process and focus their attention inward on what occurs within the therapy hour. Consequently, they are particularly concerned with preserving confidentiality, exercising caution in what is shared with other significant figures in patients' lives, and structuring those extracurricular contacts in ways that facilitate what occurs within the therapy process. In contrast, by its very nature, residential treatment is a centrifugal process. Because the main agent of treatment is the team, the more widely information is diffused and the freer and more extensive the interaction among team members, the better. Thus, the most immediate problem confronting those assuming the role of primary clinician is dealing with potential contradictions between the roles of psychotherapist and team leader.

This dilemma can be resolved in three ways. One is to subordinate the interests of the residential team to those of the psychotherapy process when conflicts arise, a strategy that may well alienate primary clinicians from the residential team and undermine the leadership that is their primary responsibility. Another is to try to establish a compromise between the interests of psychotherapy and the team. Yet, in practice, this balancing act is also likely to prove unsatisfactory. Unit staff feel they do not receive enough critical information, while patients believe too much is being revealed. No less important, clinicians may find it impossible to separate the two processes in their own minds and know when one role is affecting another. A third alternative is to accept that, except in extraordinary circumstances, the priorities of the residence take precedence over those of psychotherapy.

In the intensive short-term residential model, commitment to third option is unmistakable from the outset of treatment. Beginning with the admission interview, therapists make it clear that, although they will conduct individual psychotherapy, they are first and foremost members of the residential treatment team. Doing so is usually unnecessary since adolescents cannot help but believe that, because therapists are leaders of the team for their case, what is discussed in therapy will influence decisions about the way staff work with them on the residence and that their therapist will know much about what occurs on the unit. Lest there be any doubt, however, they are also are told that the principle of confidentiality does *not* apply to the sharing of information within the team. Primary clinicians may tell other staff anything they think will be useful and conversely bring into psychotherapy anything they learn from colleagues that could advance the treatment process. In short, it is acknowledged frankly that psychotherapy is a subordinate aspect of residential treatment as a whole.

To be sure, the ways these policies are practiced soften their impact. Just because psychotherapists are free in principle to share any information with childcare workers does not mean they cannot chose when and how much to share with whom. Moreover, with sensitive material in particular, therapists typically first work with adolescents around how staff are to be told so that they experience some control over the process. In addition, primary clinicians are helped to stay in the role of therapists when, even though they may have ultimate authority about treatment, decisions around issues of daily life are left to the unit staff. Instead of adolescents then using sessions to try to talk therapists into changes in their status, therapists can observe that adolescents must convince the team of their readiness for new responsibilities and offer to help them figure out how to do so. Primary clinicians are also spared some of the reservations therapists may have that information and advice from the therapy process may be misused. Because they also lead residential teams, they have a good deal of knowledge about and control over how ideas from the therapy process are handled, can be reasonably certain that what is shared is far more likely to be used to enhance treatment than misinterpreted or misused, and that the latter problems, when they do occur, can be corrected.

Nonetheless, such caveats do not address therapists' fundamental concerns. They do not change the facts that confidentiality does not apply to sharing information within team, that therapists can be under no illusion that they are "blank screens" upon which patients project transferences, or that their own emotional reactions to adolescents are influenced substantially by interactions with adolescents outside of therapy hours and by relationships with the rest of the clinical team.

In spite of these seeming drawbacks, accepting the primacy of the residential treatment has a number of benefits. Although therapists might wish that the scales were tilted in the other direction when the interests of psychotherapy and the residence seem to be in conflict, both they and their patients can adapt to even imperfect policies if there is reasonable justification for them and, above all, if the rules of the game are clear. More importantly, this clarity itself makes the work of the therapist easier. At the very least, the decision-making process is unambiguous, and few who work with acting-out adolescents are likely to underestimate the value of clarity and predictability in treatment structures.

THE PROBLEM OF CONFIDENTIALITY

The major reservation psychotherapists are likely to have about this solution centers on concerns about confidentiality, which has often been taken as almost a prerequisite for the conduct of psychotherapy. However, it is important to recognize that the issue of confidentiality is a practical problem, not a moral imperative or a precondition for psychotherapy.

In point of fact, the principle of confidentiality has rarely been sacrosanct in psychotherapy with children, or for that matter with adults. In working with very young children, the concept is meaningless in that extensive information is freely shared with parents, and children would not expect therapists to do otherwise. Even trying to explain confidentiality to preschoolers may be counterproductive. After all, we warn them against adults who offer to help them keep secrets from their parents. School age children and adolescents have increasing concerns about privacy, but, as has been noted, therapists frequently share a good deal of information and advice with parents (Mishne, 1983). Moreover, even with adults, confidentiality is far from absolute. Unhappily conscientious therapists must explain to patients numerous ways in which it is limited by law and by the need to obtain funding for treatment from third parties.

Given these circumstances, it is perhaps fortunate that confidentiality is not a necessary condition for therapy. In actual treatment, the overriding issue is not confidentiality, but rather trust. Patients have a right to know how information they share will be used so that they can decide what they wish to reveal. If therapists are candid about these matters, there is no violation of that trust.

From a strategic standpoint, of course, the fact that information is shared with the residential team can lead some adolescents to be reluctant to talk about sensitive material. More often than not, this loss is offset by additional sources of such material from the unit. It is rare that adolescents in good residential facilities do not share what is troubling them with some members of the team and this information can then be introduced into therapy. In any case, whether adolescents reveal what matters to them most is not based on what therapists say about confidentiality, but rather on how they act. Openness ultimately depends on adolescents' beliefs about the integrity of therapists and the residential team. Until trust is earned, they may be guarded in sharing the thoughts, feelings, and memories that trouble them, which in itself matters little. Until trust is earned, doing so is the foremost issue in treatment.

In certain respects, indicating that confidentiality does not apply within the residential team may make their work easier for psychotherapists. Many therapists believe that by trying to adhere to the principle of confidentiality as closely as possible, they keep faith with patients by protecting their right to privacy. Yet often the reverse is the case. Because therapists working with children in both inpatient and outpatient processes often share information and advice with parents and caretakers, it can be hard to tell when confidentiality has been compromised. Indicating that confidentiality does not apply within the residential team may create other complications, but at the least therapists are spared nagging doubts about when they may have crossed that ill-defined line as they share material important for a patient's welfare with caretakers.

PSYCHOTHERAPEUTIC PERSPECTIVES AND THE PROBLEM OF DUAL ROLES

The other major concern psychotherapists experience when they begin to play multiple roles is that the conditions of treatment are so changed that the rules governing therapy have been altered in fundamental, but unpredictable ways.

In certain respects, they are right. If psychotherapy is viewed as a set of concrete procedures applied according to a specific set of rules, it would be disingenuous to pretend that the process is not affected by significant changes in the context in which it is conducted. Even so, therapists are likely to be surprised at how little their day-to-day practice is altered when they assume multiple roles. Both therapists and adolescents have a capacity to compartmentalize roles when doing so is taken as a fact of life by all concerned.

Regardless, however, if approaches to psychotherapy are genuinely valuable, the most important question that can be asked is not whether they still apply to new circumstances, but rather how they apply. When the problem of dual roles in residential treatment is approached from this standpoint, psychotherapists find that they need not fear that their approaches to treatment have been compromised. Rather they are likely to discover that the theoretical orientations that have guided them as therapists are no less germane when integrating their work with that of the residential team. Indeed, each of the major approaches to psychotherapy can be readily adapted to such circumstances and provide the guidance therapists need as they adopt new modes of practice.

BEHAVIOR AND COGNITIVE-BEHAVIOR THERAPIES

Approaches to psychotherapy that involve learning particular skills and that have relatively clear-cut protocols are not deeply affected when therapists play dual roles. In practice, it may be desirable for behavior or cognitive-behavior therapists to be spared complications related to assuming a variety of functions on residential units. In principle, however, such therapies involve treatment techniques that can be utilized equally well by therapists who are responsible for other aspects of treatment. More importantly, procedures such as mastering and applying relaxation techniques, desensitization, contingency management, or identifying and correcting distorted beliefs may well be enhanced when the aid of caretakers is enlisted so that therapists receive more feedback on their effects and children can make greater use of them between therapy sessions. Rather than being an unwelcome burden, assuming the role of primary clinician may well allow therapists with such orientations to practice their art on a broader canvas.

BRIEF PSYCHOTHERAPY

Because they are founded on the same basic principles, most models of brief psychotherapy are also compatible with short-term residential treatment (Leichtman & Leichtman, 1996c). For example, in articulating "the most salient elements in brief psychotherapy" in their influential text, Budman and Gurman (1988, pp. 17-21) included: maintenance of a clear and specific focus, a high level of therapist activity, maintenance of an awareness of time, flexible use of interventions and time, and "encouragement of the patient's 'being' outside of therapy through liberal use of homework assignments, involvement of relatives and significant others in treatment, and use of 'naturally occurring' therapies in the environment." Each is fully compatible with short-term residential treatment and provides means for psychotherapists to coordinate their work with the rest of the team.

For example, intensive short-term residential treatment begins with the assumption that lengths of stay are finite and the program is organized accordingly (Leichtman & Leichtman, 1996b). With the exception of a few adolescents who may remain in the community, the time frame for the psychotherapy process is the same. Such circumstances obviously lend themselves to the adoption of time-limited approaches to psychotherapy. Moreover, as primary clinicians, therapists are time-keepers for both the residential treatment and psychotherapy processes, keeping adolescents and staff alike aware of the need to pace treatment and helping assure that their clocks are synchronized.

Because time and resources are finite, short-term residential treatment must quickly establish delimited goals and maintain "a clear and specific focus" (Leichtman & Leichtman, 1996b). Working with adolescents both in therapy and on the unit, primary clinicians are in an especially good position to determine rapidly the most critical problems to work on and to keep both therapy and residential treatment centered on them.

As team leaders as well as therapists, primary clinicians cannot help but take an active role in structuring treatment and encouraging patients to work on critical treatment issues. They also have additional leverage in this regard, since unit statuses and other tangible rewards are tied to such work. Similarly, as leaders of residential teams, primary clinicians already apply many of the techniques Budman and Gurman (1988, pp. 18-19) recommend for encouraging "being" outside therapy. The various tasks that comprise the residential treatment program already provide adolescents with a host of assignments between sessions, few "others" are more significant than their parents, members of the residential team, and peers on the unit who are all actively involved in the residential treatment process, and the rest of the residential treatment program itself comprises a host of "naturally occurring therapies."

In short, there is an inherent synergy between short-term residential treatment and brief psychotherapy which primary clinicians by virtue of their dual roles are ideally situated to exploit.

SUPPORTIVE PSYCHOTHERAPY

As noted, therapists with psychodynamic orientations are likely to have the greatest reservations about assuming multiple roles because of concerns about its effects on the production of sensitive material in psychotherapy and on manifestations of transference and countertransference. Yet these concerns are related chiefly to expressive psychotherapy and psychoanalysis, processes in which interpreting unconscious motivations and working through transferences are critical. Other forms of psychodynamic therapy, ones that may be especially germane for the types of children and adolescents who are referred for residential treatment, are less adversely affected and may even be facilitated by the combination of roles.

Although psychoanalysts always had some recognition of the importance of supportive techniques (Rockland, 1989), by the early 1950s, many had come to doubt that psychoanalysis and expressive psychotherapy were appropriate for most patients with severe character disorders and psychotic conditions. In such cases, the uncovering of conflicts and the appearance of primitive transferences often led to marked acting out, regression, and disorganization. As a consequence, with the emergence of ego psychology, psychoanalysts such as Bibring (1954), Gill (1951), and Alexander (1961) articulated a rationale for supportive psychotherapy and techniques for its application. Over the succeeding decades, this form of treatment continued to be a major, if unheralded aspect of the practice of psychodynamic psychotherapy (Dewald, 1971; Rockland, 1989; Wallerstein, 1986; Werman, 1984).

Authorities on supportive psychotherapy stress four characteristics that set it apart from expressive techniques. *First*, the goal of therapy is not to unearth and interpret unconscious conflict, but rather to strengthen ego functions and improve adaptation. *Second*, the material that therapists seek to elicit in each process is different. Expressive techniques (e.g., the use of the couch, neutrality, free association, the privileged position of dreams, and the therapist's attitudes in general) are intended to help clients relax defenses, move beyond preoccupation with exigencies of day-to-day living, give voice to primary process ideation, foster transference reactions, and recall memories of childhood. In contrast, supportive techniques focus on the "here and now" rather than the past, adaptation to "the real world" rather than indulgence in fantasy, and secondary process thinking rather than more primitive forms of ideation. *Third,* comparable differences characterize the relationship with therapist. In psychoanalysis, the most expressive form of therapy, therapists limit their interaction with patients, adopt a neutral stance, and even seek to act like "a blank screen" in order to foster the emergence of transference. In contrast, in supportive psychotherapy, therapists try to remain "real figures" and discourage intense transference reactions, favor active involvement with patients rather than disciplined passivity, renounce "neutrality" in order to foster adaptive actions, and abandon abstinence and offer emotional support, positive relationships, and "corrective emotional experiences." Although the transference phenomena that inevitably arise are not ignored, therapists typically tacitly accept and make use of their positive aspects, finesse negative aspects, and confront negative transference only when it threatens to undermine the treatment relationship. *Finally,* in expressive psychotherapy, especially psychoanalysis, interpretation of unconscious conflicts is the preeminent technique, while a host of other interventions including advice, persuasion, and education through which therapists may influence patients are recognized, yet treated as modifications of the "parameters" of therapy that are to be indulged in with caution. In supportive therapies that hierarchy is reversed. Therapists make liberal use of techniques such as "corrective emotional experience" (e.g., providing some of the kind of parenting patients appear to need), offering emotional support, role-modeling, helping with reality testing as needed, advising, teaching psychological and social skills, and encouraging or discouraging particular behavior both overtly and covertly. In short, interpretation of unconscious conflict is limited if not eschewed and therapists adopt whatever other techniques show promise of facilitating adaptation and strengthening defenses.

Far from posing serious questions about therapists playing multiple roles in residential treatment, the assumptions underlying supportive psychotherapy are, in fact, compatible with doing so. The overriding goals of both processes are the same, fostering healthy development and adaptation. In principle, there are no conflicts in tasks upon which primary clinicians work as therapists and team leaders. The issues with which supportive therapists are most concerned, the salient problems in daily living with which youngsters are struggling, are the very ones that preoccupy residential staff. The fact that primary clinicians play a "real role" in clients' lives, typically that of a parental figure trying to help them negotiate basic developmental tasks, is consistent with the role of therapists in supportive psychotherapy. And, finally, most of the techniques of supportive psychotherapy are those used by others on the residential team as well. When therapists consult to staff around them and coordinate both treatment processes, the effectiveness of each is increased. Hence, far from contraindicating adoption of multiple roles in residential treatment, the literature on supportive psychotherapy can provide psychotherapists with guidance and how to do so.

EXPRESSIVE PSYCHOTHERAPY

Of all approaches in psychotherapy, expressive psychodynamic ones would appear to be those most compromised by psychotherapists assuming multiple roles. Yet this perspective, too, can make significant contributions to psychotherapy in short-term residential treatment. To appreciate how it can do so, it is helpful to take a step back and consider the altered relationship with therapist in such treatment.

If therapists do only psychotherapy, how critical issues such as transference and countertransference and, indeed, how treatment itself are conceptualized can be understood chiefly in terms of what occurs within the session. When psychotherapists have numerous other contacts with clients and share information with and direct a clinical team, it would be absurd to believe that there are two separate relationships with the primary clinician–one as therapist, the other as team leader–or that what occurs in psychotherapy is unaffected by a host of other contacts and relationships. Rather, if psychotherapy is fully integrated with residential treatment, there is one process with different aspects. What occurs between adolescents and therapists at all times is part of the therapy process, even if it is discussed chiefly during therapy hours; therapists always remain leaders of clinical teams even when meeting alone with patients to "do psychotherapy." No less important, if there is thorough integration of the two processes, everything occurring on the residential unit becomes part of the psychotherapy process in the sense that information is exchanged freely between the therapist and the unit staff and staff become part of the therapy process insofar as the therapist functions as team leader, offering recommendations for interventions on the unit and using staff as surrogates at times.

When this perspective is adopted, many of the problems involved in using a psychodynamic perspective fade. Confidentiality in the therapy process does apply to the basic treatment unit, the team. Material open for exploration and interpretation expands, since it now includes not only that shared with the therapist, but also with the team. Transference to therapists may be muted and murky because of their "real roles" and their active involvement in many aspects of adolescents' lives, yet transference reactions are manifested in striking forms in relationships with caretakers on the unit who have assumed parental roles. Similarly, therapists' readings of countertransference reactions in themselves may be complicated by contacts with patients and caretakers outside of therapy hours, yet again the understanding and interpretation of countertransference can now include the reactions of other members of the team. As anyone involved in the residential treatment of deeply disturbed adolescents can attest, such reactions are so much part of work in these settings and often so dramatic that therapists never need fear being without such material. Also, as most supervisors can attest, countertransference reactions are often far easier to recognize in others than oneself. Finally, not only is it possible to address such material from a psychodynamic perspective within therapy hours, but, insofar as therapists direct residential teams, interpreting and working through dynamic issues need not be confined to therapy hours alone but can now occur throughout the day.

Applications of psychoanalytic perspectives of this kind, it should be noted, are hardly unprecedented. They bear a clear resemblance to that of Kernberg (1973), although he described programs that maintained a greater separation of psychotherapy and hospital treatment. There are also similarities to Bettelheim's approach to milieu therapy, which carried the amalgamation of roles even further (Bettelheim & Saunders, 1979).

CONCLUSION

Some psychotherapists may find the views of how traditional modes of practice can be utilized in a primary clinician model sufficiently familiar that the ideas advanced here hardly seem novel. Others may suspect differences in practice have been unduly minimized to defend a course of treatment that may seem questionable. For the present purposes, neither point need be debated. It is perhaps sufficient to recognize that, in serving as primary clinicians, psychotherapists do assume an unfamiliar role and are faced with new challenges, but they also bring to that role perspectives and therapeutic skills that can be adapted to meet those challenges. At this point, matters of general theory become less important than considerations of how those theories are translated into actual practice.

REFERENCES

Alexander, F. (1961). *The scope of psychoanalysis*. New York: Basic Books.

Bettelheim, B. & Sanders, J. (1979). Milieu therapy: The Orthogenic School model. In J. A. Noshpitz (Ed.), *Basic handbook of child psychiatry: Vol. 3. Therapeutic interventions* (pp. 216-230). New York: Basic Books.

Bibring, E. (1954). Psychoanalysis and dynamic psychotherapies. *Journal of the American Psychoanalytic Association, 2*, 745-770.

Budman, S. H. & Gurman, A. S. (1988). *Theory and practice of brief psychotherapy*. New York: Guilford.

Dewald, P. (1971). *Psychotherapy: A dynamic approach*. New York: Basic Books.

Gill, M. M. (1951). Ego psychology and psychotherapy. *Psychoanalytic Quarterly, 20*, 62-71.

Kernberg, O. (1973). Toward an integrative theory of hospital treatment. *The Annual of Psychoanalysis, 1*, 363-388.

Leichtman, M. & Leichtman, M. L. (1996a). A model of short-term residential treatment: I. The nature of the challenge. In C. Waller (Ed.), *Contributions to residential treatment 1996* (pp. 85-92). Alexandria, VA: American Association of Children's Residential Centers.

Leichtman, M. & Leichtman, M. L. (1996b). A model of short-term residential treatment: II. General principles. In C. Waller (Ed.), *Contributions to residential treatment 1996* (pp. 93-102). Alexandria, VA: American Association of Children's Residential Centers.

Leichtman, M. & Leichtman, M. L. (1996c). A model of short-term residential treatment: III. Changing roles. In C. Waller (Ed.), *Contributions to residential treatment 1996* (pp. 103-109). Alexandria, VA: American Association of Children's Residential Centers.

Monahan, R.T. (1989). Individual and group psychotherapy. In R. D. Lyman, S. Prentice-Dunn, & S. Gabel (Eds.), *Residential and inpatient treatment of children and adolescents* (pp. 191-205). New York: Plenum Press.

Redl, F. & Wineman, D. (1957). *The aggressive child*. Glencoe, IL: The Free Press.

Rockland, L. H. (1989). *Supportive psychotherapy: A psychodynamic approach*. New York: Basic Books.

Stamm, I. (1989). A psychoanalytic model. In R. D. Lyman, S. Prentice-Dunn, & S. Gabel (Eds.), *Residential and inpatient treatment of children and adolescents* (pp. 25-42). New York: Plenum Press.

Stone, L.A. (1979). Residential treatment. In J. D. Noshpitz (Ed.), *Basic handbook of child psychiatry: Vol. 3. Therapeutic interventions* (pp. 231-262). New York: Basic Books.

Trieschman, A. E., Whittaker, J. K., & Brendtro, L. K. (1969). *The other 23 hours*. Chicago: Aldine Publishing Company.

Wallerstein, R. S. (1986). *Forty-two lives in treatment: A study of psychoanalysis and psychotherapy*. New York: Brunner/Mazel.

Werman, D. S. (1984). *The practice of supportive psychotherapy*. New York: Brunner/Mazel.

BIOGRAPHICAL NOTES

Martin Leichtman, PhD, directed a residential treatment unit in the Child and Adolescent Unit of the Menninger Clinic and has served on the faculties of the Karl Menninger School of Mental Health Services and the Topeka Institute for Psychoanalysis.

Maria Luisa Leichtman, PhD, has served as Director of Residential Treatment at the Menninger Clinic.

The Integration of Psychotherapy and Residential Treatment in an Intensive Short-Term Treatment Program: Part III. Implementation as Therapy Begins

Martin Leichtman, PhD
Maria Luisa Leichtman, PhD

SUMMARY. This paper explores ways in which a high degree of integration of psychotherapy and residential treatment can be realized in clinical practice. Describing a model of intensive short-term residential treatment used in the Menninger Clinic Child and Adolescent Service between 1993 and 2001, it first examines the role of the primary clinician in relation to the residential team and then considers the ways in which integration of psychotherapy and residential treatment was implemented in the initial stage of the treatment process. *[Article copies available for a fee from The Haworth Document Delivery Service: 1-800-HAWORTH. E-mail address: <docdelivery@haworthpress. com> Website: <http://www.HaworthPress.com> © 2003 by The Haworth Press, Inc. All rights reserved.]*

KEYWORDS. Beginning phase of treatment, clinical interview, treatment plans, DSM-IV diagnoses, treatment contract

The authors may be written at: The Foxhill Medical Building, 4601 West 109th Street–Suite 240, Overland Park, KS 66211.

[Haworth co-indexing entry note]: "The Integration of Psychotherapy and Residential Treatment in an Intensive Short-Term Treatment Program: Part III. Implementation as Therapy Begins." Leichtman, Martin, and Maria Luisa Leichtman. Co-published simultaneously in *Residential Treatment for Children & Youth* (The Haworth Press, Inc.) Vol. 20, No. 4, 2003, pp. 95-106; and: *Psychotherapy in Group Care: Making Life Good Enough* (ed: D. Patrick Zimmerman et al.) The Haworth Press, Inc., 2003, pp. 95-106. Single or multiple copies of this article are available for a fee from The Haworth Document Delivery Service [1-800-HAWORTH, 9:00 a.m. - 5:00 p.m. (EST). E-mail address: docdelivery@haworthpress.com].

http://www.haworthpress.com/store/product.asp?sku=J007
© 2003 by The Haworth Press, Inc. All rights reserved.
10.1300/J007v20n04_07

INTRODUCTION

Focusing on structural and theoretical issues, the preceding papers sought to show how adoption of a primary clinician model can afford a high degree of integration of psychotherapy and residential treatment. This paper explores ways in which that promise can be realized in clinical practice. Describing a model of intensive short-term residential treatment used in the Menninger Clinic Child and Adolescent Service between 1993 and 2001, it first examines the role of the primary clinician in relation to the residential team and then considers the ways in which integration of psychotherapy and residential treatment was implemented in the initial stage of the treatment process.

THE TREATMENT CONTEXT

The Menninger Residential Treatment Program consisted of two 12-bed units that were designed to provide services comparable to those of intermediate and long-term hospitals for severely disturbed adolescents. Each unit was directed by a clinical psychologist who also was primary clinician for 5 to 7 adolescents. A staff psychologist, psychology postdoctoral fellows, and psychiatric residents served as primary clinicians for the rest of the patients. The residents also handled the medications of adolescents on the units under the supervision of a child psychiatrist. Other members of the residential team included childcare workers and nurses, who were responsible for the day-to-day care of adolescents (Leichtman, 2001; Leichtman & Leichtman, 1996), social workers and social work trainees, who worked with families (Cafferty & Leichtman, 2001; Leichtman & Leichtman, 1996), and a substance abuse counselor, who provided individual counseling and groups for both units (Leichtman & Leichtman, 2002b). In addition, adolescents in the program attended an on-grounds therapeutic school, had access to other Menninger programs providing specialized groups for eating disorders or trauma, and made extensive use of community schools, churches, job training workshops, and 12-step groups (Leichtman & Leichtman, 2002a).

Primary clinicians were given a 4-hour weekly allocation for each of their cases. They could allot this time flexibly, but as a rule about 40% was used for formal psychotherapy (usually a half hour and an hour session each week) and informal therapy contacts as needed. The remainder was devoted to: (1) groups (two group psychotherapy sessions and one community meeting weekly); (2) case management (e.g., diagnostic conferences, three team meetings a week to review each youngster on the unit for 10 to 15 minutes as well as address salient issues on the residence, a staff meeting to focus on issues of team functioning and adolescents who presented special problems for staff, and contacts with other team members to exchange information and coordinate treatment); and (3) administrative responsibilities such as admission, diagnostic, and discharge reports, treatment plans, and contacts with family, managed care reviewers, and clinicians who had referred clients or to whom they would be referred. Although this workload could be heavy, the fact that clinicians had many cases on the unit that proceeded at different paces allowed for economical use of time and the opportunity to balance the workload over extended periods.

CRITICAL ISSUES IN THE BEGINNING PHASE OF TREATMENT

In residential treatment, psychotherapy, and indeed therapy of any kind, the first phase of treatment consists of five basic tasks. First, patients must learn the structure of the treatment process, the rules of the game that provide the framework for therapy. Second, adolescents must develop a trust in treaters sufficient to accept that structure, even if at times they may stretch or even substantially bend its rules. Third, within the context of those rules and relationships, patients must communicate through their words and their behavior the nature of the problems that brought them to treatment, the resources they draw upon to solve those problems, and ways therapists can help them do so. Fourth, bringing their experience and expertise to bear on this information, treaters must formulate a diagnostic picture that clarifies the nature of the problems, their probable causes, and, above all, approaches that can be taken to their solution. And, finally, therapists must enter into a dialogue around these findings with patients, in this case both adolescents and their families, that further clarifies problems and leads to agreement on a treatment plan. Such agreements may involve agreeing to disagree about aspects of that plan for a period of time. Once these tasks are accomplished the first phase of treatment is complete.

THE INITIAL INTERVIEW

The short-term residential treatment process begins with an intake interview with adolescents and their parents at the time of admission. The interview is conducted chiefly by the primary clinician, but the social worker, and representatives of the nursing and childcare staff are also present and participate, asking questions or providing information whenever they think it appropriate.

The interview has two purposes. First, it is used to articulate the problems that brought youngsters and their families to treatment. Typically, at the outset, children and their parents describe and often enact those problems and explain why residential treatment has been necessary in spite of earlier outpatient treatments and brief hospitalizations. These matters are explored sufficiently to arrive at a preliminary diagnosis and treatment plan. Second, the interview provides both adolescents and their parents with an introduction to the structure of the residential program. Information is offered about the rules of the unit, the types of treatment available, and basic expectations of clients and their families. Unit staff later review these points with adolescents in greater detail (again and again); parents learn more about them in subsequent meetings with the social worker; and both adolescents and their families are given a handbook which allows them to process the information over time.

As is generally the case with therapy, the form of this interview is as important as its content. From the first, primary clinicians function both as therapists conducting a diagnostic interview and leaders of residential teams. Adolescents are not only told that critical information from the therapy process will be shared with the team, but its members are also present as sensitive material is elicited. The fact that the program will heavily emphasize collaborative work with families is underscored by their inclusion as well. Surprisingly, insofar as therapists act on the assumption that it is important for parents and staff to know about the seriousness of symptoms, most adolescents are remarkably candid in describing them. The interview may be the first time parents learn the full extent of the suicidal ideation, self-injurious behavior, drug use, hallucinations, or other problems troubling their children. Because of the public nature of this forum, adolescents may hold back some personal material until later individual sessions with the therapist, especially around sexual issues. However, the structure of the initial interview gives them fair warning of the degree to which treatment will involve a group process that emphasizes sharing information and treatment responsibilities with the residential staff, parents, and, later, peers.

EARLY THERAPY SESSIONS

In addition to forming relationships with adolescents, primary clinicians have two principal tasks during the first two weeks of individual psychotherapy. These tasks are a continuation of those begun in the admission interview.

The first consists of helping adolescents understand and adjust to the structure of residential treatment process and, above all, facilitating their use of the residential team. Work around these issues is relatively easy to initiate because of a convergence of adolescents' interests and what primary clinicians have to offer. On one side, coming to terms with the regimented, rule-bound structure of unit life and gaining increasing freedom are among adolescents' most immediate short-term goals, and getting out of treatment and returning home are often chief among their long-term goals. On the other side, staff decisions about privileges on the unit and ultimately about discharge are based heavily on adolescents demonstrating that they can follow rules, handle increasing responsibilities, and manage critical aspects of daily living such as school, peer relationships, and interactions with their families. Although primary clinicians have ultimate responsibility for treatment, much of the decision-making regarding day-to-day life on the unit and home visits is delegated to childcare staff, social workers, and parents. Moreover, those decisions are not only based on overt behavior such as following rules, but also on staff and parents understanding what adolescents are thinking and feeling so that they are comfortable allowing them increasing responsibility. Hence, as therapists, primary clinicians can adopt the role of coaches, teaching adolescents about negotiating "the system" and about the behavior and relationships necessary to achieve those ends.

For example, because many adolescents are referred for residential treatment because of suicidal ideation and gestures, self-injury, assaultiveness, running away, or other serious forms of acting out, all begin on highly restricted statuses in which they are confined to the unit for the first few days and subsequently go off to the cafeteria and school in other buildings only when accompanied one-to-one by staff members. Even the modest raise of status necessary to participate in group activities on grounds requires earning the trust of the childcare staff as a group. To do so, adolescents must not only refrain from acting out, but also talk with all workers about the immediate problems that necessitated residential treatment and convince them that the problems can be handled without constant close monitoring. They need not act as if wishes to harm themselves, run away, or blow-up are no longer present. To the contrary, doing so would be unrealistic and elicit suspicion no matter how well they behaved. Rather adolescents are expected to tell workers about what these urges have been like, when they occur, how they are being managed, and how staff can be of help with them in times of crisis. When initial therapy sessions are used to understand these expectations and think about how to explain problems to childcare workers, therapists begin to build an alliance by helping adolescents achieve more freedom and privileges. In addition, the work of the psychotherapy process is facilitated because adolescents often find it easier to talk with therapists about affect-laden topics and experience a greater sense of control when issues are approached indirectly from the standpoint of how to discuss them with third parties.

This opening gambit is paradigmatic of the ways in which basic social and adaptational tasks can be approached in therapy throughout treatment. At each stage, adolescents have an interest in getting more unit privileges, which are also steps toward discharge. Those privileges are based largely on increasing mastery of symptoms and age-appropriate developmental tasks *and* convincing caretakers–both childcare workers and parents–that they can be trusted with greater independence. Hence, from the first, therapists can assume a role that involves helping adolescents develop new skills and manage relationships with significant figures in their lives in ways that enable them to achieve these ends.

The second basic psychotherapeutic task, that which occupies the bulk of the initial sessions, consists of conducting rigorous diagnostic interviews. Emphasizing that major decisions will be made about treatment at a team conference at the end of the second week, therapists focus on gathering information about adolescents' histories, their major symptoms, their patterns of thinking, their modes of managing affect and regulating behavior, their experience of themselves and significant figures in their lives, their attitudes toward school and work, their interests and talents, their goals for the future, and their thoughts about treatment. In keeping with the focused, time-limited nature of short-term treatment, the necessity of making decisions at the diagnostic conference provides a common task and a deadline that require active work on the part of both adolescents and therapists. The need to collaborate, the task itself (learning about adolescents' history and current life), and the necessity of discussing material in order to present it to third parties often allows a remarkable amount of significant information to be gathered in a brief period and contributes to the more rapid formation of a therapeutic alliance.

SHARING DIAGNOSTIC FINDINGS
AND CRYSTALLIZING TREATMENT PLANS

At the diagnostic conference, information from a variety of sources is reviewed. In addition to the primary clinicians' interviews, there are a detailed developmental history and assessment of family issues, medical reports, psychological testing, an education evaluation, an activities assessment, a substance abuse evaluation, observations of nursing and childcare staff, and reports from consultants about specialized problems such as eating disorders or trauma. On the basis of the team's discussion of this data, the primary clinician formulates a diagnosis, identifies the etiological factors that appear to be responsible for the problems, and articulates a comprehensive, but still tentative treatment plan that includes consideration of length of stay and probable discharge plans.

Typically, the conference findings and how to present them to parents are discussed with patients at the next therapy session. The findings and what adolescents have added to them are reviewed with the family as a whole soon thereafter. This process of sharing findings is the focal point of the first phase of both psychotherapy and residential treatment since it enables adolescents, their parents, and the clinical team to consolidate their understanding of problems and provides a framework for working on them together in the succeeding phases of treatment.

A useful format for these sessions with both psychotherapy and family sessions is one that focuses on four basic sets of issues that were central to the diagnostic conference. Discussion is invited about each before proceeding to the next.

The natural starting point is a brief review of the specific problems that brought the adolescent to treatment. These problems are ones that adolescents and parents described at the admission interview, now supplemented by information that they have added and issues the team has recognized in subsequent meetings. Beginning with an agreement on these problems is critical because the overriding diagnostic task is understanding them, the purpose of treatment is developing strategies for managing them, and the criterion for discharge is arriving at a point at which adolescents and families can manage them sufficiently well that they can work on them in outpatient programs.

A second set of issues discussed are formal DSM-IV diagnoses. Although many clinicians involved in residential treatment have reservations about "labeling children," they are often required to do so, adolescents and their families are curious about those diagnoses, and patients are entitled to know critical information that is part of their written records and shared with other professionals and third parties. More important, diagnoses are tools for organizing information, prioritizing problems, and planning treatment that can be as useful for families as they are for clinicians. For many adolescents and parents having a label affords a sense of beginning to understanding problems. At first, this may be an exercise in magical thinking, but it ceases to be so if reading about syndromes and their treatment is encouraged and in some cases even required. When patients do so, far from feeling strange or different, they may now recognize that their problems are shared by millions of other people, that those problems are comprehensible, and that there are a variety of recognized treatments for them. Moreover, even if they do not agree with diagnoses or approaches to their treatment, such information invites an active dialogue around the issues rather than passive acceptance of or resistance to treatments they question.

To minimize misunderstandings, discussions of diagnoses can start with a number of caveats. First and foremost, it should be stressed that labels are ways of describing groups of behaviors, that over the years mental health professions have often changed the names and groupings of symptoms and will no doubt continue to do in the future, and that it is the behavior rather than the labels that is important. Second, the labels refer to symptoms, to problems people experience; they do not define who individuals are. Third, with many adolescents, the diagnoses are tentative and, at best, heuristic tools for describing current functioning. Clinicians who wish to offer diagnoses with a greater degree of assurance and ones that will not be subject to change over time would be well advised to work with adults, whose character and pathology have crystallized and with whom problems have often recurred a number of times.

Because adolescents who are referred for residential treatment have numerous problems and because diagnoses are intended to be used descriptively to orient families to treatment, we typically favor multiple categories. Those that are easiest to apply and least controversial are Axis I disorders. Anxiety and affective disorders, AD/HD, learning problems, and substance abuse, for example, are all based on overt, recognizable behavior and tied to specific treatment approaches. In addition, we give Parent-Child Relational Problem diagnoses in most cases in order to stress that we are concerned not only in working with adolescents but also with their parents. Such diagnoses are not hard to justify. Family dysfunction is a significant contributing factor to the serious pathologies that necessitate residential treatment and, even when it is not, such pathologies can take such a toll on family life that they produce "relational problems." This diagnosis is, of course, notoriously vague. Yet, that very vagueness allows social workers to specify "the relational problems" in terms of the issues that children and their parents have described and enacted in the course of the evaluation and that must be addressed if adolescents are to return home. We also use both formal Axis II diagnoses and notations about traits in a liberal fashion. Although many clinicians are reluctant to use such diagnoses with adolescents, patients often require residential treatment either because of characterological problems or because of ways those problems affect the treatment of Axis I disorders. More important, residential treatment is especially concerned with "enduring patterns" of "cognition, affectivity, interpersonal functioning, and impulse control" (American Psychiatric Association, 1994, p. 275). For all of their shortcomings, DSM-IV personality disorder categories help orient adolescents and families to the treatment of these problems as well.

In discussing diagnoses related to personality, we have found that it is important to deal with three sets of issues. First, the pejorative nature of diagnoses should be addressed. For example, after noting only half jokingly that the problem with DSM-IV is that it implies that one either has a personality disorder or no personality at all, it can be stressed that the labels are being used as a way of trying to describe patterns of thinking, managing affect and behavior, and relating to others. Second, syndromes should be described in ways adolescents and families can understand and in the process humanized. For example, few teenagers like being called "histrionic" or even know what it means. However, many can recognize that they are dramatic, emotional individuals, that getting attention by being attractive and appealing is terribly important to them, and that they so badly need to feel close to others that they often act like "people pleasers" or go to desperate lengths to hold on to relationships that are bad for them. Indeed, when it is observed that, in the face of crises, people with histrionic characteristics act like they are living lives out of a soap opera or are characters on *Beverly Hills 90210*, the label may even become a source of pride. Finally, although parents and adolescents usually recognize the behavior that results in personality disorder diagnoses, those criteria read like an extended list of misbehavior and character flaws. It can be stressed that these conditions are efforts at adaptation, many of which have positive aspects however problematic their consequences. For example, with borderline conditions, particular emphasis can be placed on the centrality of efforts to establish and maintain relationships and ways in which many of the symptoms reflect either desperate efforts to hold on to attachments or expressions of anxiety, anger, or despair as these fail.

Having outlined problems in this way, it is natural to consider next how they have arisen. By integrating information from diagnostic reports and focusing on events parents and children have described as especially salient in their lives, primary clinicians can give an account of possible genetic and constitutional factors contributing to problems and an overview of how temperament, family dynamics, and major stressors may have affected the child's personality, their management of basic developmental tasks, and the problems with which they are currently struggling in major phases of childhood and adolescence. In order to deal with sensitivities to blame, it is useful to approach such explanations from the standpoint of why, given the child's endowment, the family's history, and the stressors with which they have struggled, it is natural that such problems would have arisen. It is also important to recognize as much as possible the strengths and accomplishments of children and families in spite of those problems. When these explanations are handled skillfully, adolescents and parents do not usually find them new or surprising, but rather feel that they bring together and organize the material that they have described in ways that recognize issues they have long sensed, but had difficulty articulating.

The fact that such explanations are tentative and, at times, quite speculative need not be a problem. When primary clinicians acknowledge that they may well have a clear understanding of the factors responsible for problems only at the end of treatment rather than at the beginning, initial formulations can be presented as hypotheses which they would like adolescents and their families to help revise. Indeed, it can be noted that doing so may be an important task of therapy and family work throughout the course of treatment. What is valuable about such diagnostic pictures is that they serve as a means of presenting an integrated overview of findings from disparate diagnostic reports, and help patients and families place their problems in perspective. Even more important, insofar as thoughts about possible causes of problems point to ways of addressing them, these formulations provide a rationale for treatment plans.

Typically, the range of problems that have brought adolescents to treatment, the multiple diagnoses that have been noted, and the integrated picture of biological, psychological, and social factors contributing to them provide a framework for appreciating a comprehensive, multimodal treatment plan. With most patients those plans include medications and learning to manage them, psychotherapy, group therapy, family therapy, and social skills groups. With many, they also include specialized counseling and groups for substance abuse, and for some, specialized programs for problems around eating or trauma. Because residential treatment emphasizes the importance of fostering healthy development and building upon adolescents' interests and talents, treatment plans also give extensive attention to active engagement in family activities, establishing and maintaining friendships, doing well in school, learning vocational skills, pursing hobbies and recreational interests, and involvement in community activities (Leichtman & Leichtman, 2002a). It is adolescents' success in the latter aspects of treatment as much as their response to formal psychiatric treatments that demonstrate to them and others their readiness to return home.

On the basis of discussions of these issues, revisions are made in the diagnostic picture and recommendations and the treatment plan is finalized.

"THE CONTRACT"

The last task of the first phase of treatment is that of incorporating diagnosis into the treatment process on the residence. Participation of members of some childcare workers at the conference and sharing of conference findings with others at team meetings provide ways of using the diagnostic picture to inform staff interventions with adolescents on the unit. In addition, adolescents often discuss what they have learned about their conditions with peers and staff at meetings on the unit or in group therapy. Some do so in order to question and even ridicule the conference findings; many are genuinely interested in sharing what they have learned with peers; and some, having watched experienced patients talk about problems at such meetings, are simply glad that they now have a script that will allow them to do so as well. From the standpoint of treatment, what is important is that, whether or not the adolescents accept diagnoses and treatment plans, they now enter into serious discussions of them with unit staff and peers as well as with therapists.

The process of bringing diagnosis and treatment planning into the unit at a level peers and staff can understand and work with is institutionalized in the form of a rite of passage, "The Contract," which new patients must complete in order to move beyond the most basic unit status. Given to them shortly after their admission, the contract consists of a single sheet of paper with four tasks: listing and describing their strengths and problems, those of their family, the history of the problems that brought them to treatment, and the major goals that need to be accomplished in treatment. Adolescents must first produce a draft of the contract themselves, although with limited youngsters or those with learning disabilities childcare workers may do the writing and even help formulate ideas. The draft is next discussed in detail with the primary clinician, the social worker, and several childcare workers, all of whom raise questions about omissions and points that appear unclear, impractical, or less than candid. Treaters do not sign the document until they are satisfied that adolescents have made a genuine effort to describe the problems that brought them to treatment and serious goals for themselves. Because the contract is discussed in therapy while information is being gathered for the diagnostic conference, the primary clinician can coach patients on how to incorporate that information into the contract and discussions with staff and peers. Conversely, the goals patients articulate in the contract can be used in developing their treatment plans.

After revisions are made and the necessary signatures obtained, the contract is presented at a community meeting attended by all patients and staff. Adolescents read the document to the group and then answer questions from them. Because peers have had a chance to get to know newcomers and their problems are presented in a systematic way, other patients are often ready to inquire about their lives in detail at this time. Living in a culture that heavily emphasizes the concept of a therapeutic community, peers are typically supportive of adolescents who have been honest, but challenge those who are guarded, superficial, or oppositional more vigorously than staff. Primary clinicians, who are present at these meetings, can often help keep their patients and the group focused on critical issues, making discussions more productive and further coordinating psychotherapeutic and residential aspects of the treatment process.

With the diagnostic conference, the sharing of its results with adolescent and their families, and the presentation of the contract, the initial phase of therapy is complete. Adolescents and their families now understand the structure of the treatment process; they have formed working relationships with treaters; and problems and plans for addressing them have been defined and agreed upon. They also have a sense of the emphasis placed on integrating psychotherapy with the work of the residence. From the first, they can see the extent to which members of the team maintain close working relationships, to which information is freely exchanged, and to which the tasks of the residence are brought into the psychotherapy process and those of the psychotherapy process are fed back into residential treatment.

REFERENCES

American Psychiatric Association (1994). *Diagnostic criteria from DSM-IV*. Washington, DC.

Cafferty, H. & Leichtman, M. (2001). Facilitating the transition from residential treatment into the community: II. Changing social work roles. *Residential Treatment for Children & Youth, 19(2)*, 13-25.

Leichtman, M. (2001). Facilitating the transition from residential treatment into the community: III. Changing roles of nursing and child care staff. *Residential Treatment for Children & Youth, 19(2)*, 27-37.

Leichtman, M. & Leichtman, M. L. (1996). A model of short-term residential treatment: III. Changing roles. In C. Waller (Ed.), *Contributions to residential treatment 1996* (pp. 103-109). Alexandria, VA: American Association of Children's Residential Centers.

Leichtman, M. & Leichtman, M. L. (2002a). Facilitating the transition from residential treatment into the community: IV. Making use of community resources. *Residential Treatment for Children & Youth, 19(3)*, 43-52.

Leichtman, M. & Leichtman, M. L. (2002b). Facilitating the transition from residential treatment into the community: V. Substance abuse programs. *Residential Treatment for Children & Youth, 19(4)*, 31-37.

BIOGRAPHICAL NOTES

Martin Leichtman, PhD, directed a residential treatment unit in the Child and Adolescent Unit of the Menninger Clinic and has served on the faculties of the Karl Menninger School of Mental Health Services and the Topeka Institute for Psychoanalysis.

Maria Luisa Leichtman, PhD, has served as Director of Residential Treatment at the Menninger Clinic.

Index

**Indianapolis
Marion County
Public Library**

Renew by Phone
269-5222

Renew on the Web
www.imcpl.org

For general Library information
please call 269-1700.